SILENT DIPLOMACY

Hidden Forces Shaping the World

Shah Rukh

CONTENTS

INTRODUCTION

In the complex tapestry of international relations, where power dynamics, alliances, and strategic maneuvering define the global stage, there exists a realm often obscured from public view — the realm of silent diplomacy. This book, "Silent Diplomacy: Hidden Forces Shaping the World," embarks on a profound exploration into the clandestine corridors of global affairs, unveiling the hidden forces and intricate machinations that shape the destiny of nations.

As the title suggests, this journey into silent diplomacy invites readers to navigate the unseen chessboard of geopolitics, where the most consequential moves are made with discretion and strategic foresight. Beyond the diplomatic handshakes and public declarations lie covert alliances, intricate networks, and the subtle language of influence that weave together the fabric of international relations. It is within these shadows that hidden tensions simmer, cultural influences echo, and technological forces silently revolutionize the geopolitical landscape.

Our exploration begins with an understanding of the historical roots that have shaped the practice of silent diplomacy. From the secret negotiations of ancient civilizations to the nuanced strategies employed during the Cold War, history serves as our guide to decipher the origins of hidden forces at play. We delve into the geopolitical chess games of the past, where nations employed silent resilience to navigate crises, proxy conflicts, and the ever-shifting alliances that define the world order.

Moving beyond history, we illuminate the contemporary landscape where silent diplomacy is omnipresent, influencing everything from economic negotiations to intelligence sharing. We dissect the economic espionage, cybernetic frontiers, and covert alliances that define the modern era, illustrating the enduring relevance of silent forces in shaping the trajectory of global dynamics.

Throughout these pages, we unravel the whispers in the corridors of power, where subtle language and soft power become tools of influence. We explore the veiled agendas that underlie diplomatic interactions, decoding the strategic intentions that guide the actions of nations. As we journey further, we encounter the echo of history, understanding how the persistent impact of historical events continues to reverberate through the corridors of global affairs.

In the chapters that follow, the book meticulously explores topics ranging from undercurrents of conflict and the silent handshake of covert alliances to the silent observers who navigate the intelligence landscape. We decipher the silent code of diplomatic language, unravel the societal changes brought about by technological forces, and examine the delicate equilibrium of power that constitutes the balancing acts of nations on the global stage.

Our exploration is not confined to the actions of states alone. We shine a light on the role of non-state actors, the influence of international organizations, and the silent architects who craft the geopolitical landscape. The intricate interplay of cultural influences on diplomacy, the strategic use of soft power, and the secretive negotiations behind closed doors all find their place in the comprehensive tapestry of silent diplomacy.

As we journey through these pages, readers will gain a profound understanding of the covert alliances, unseen forces, and hidden strategies that underpin the world's geopolitical theater. "Silent

Diplomacy: Hidden Forces Shaping the World" seeks to peel back the layers of diplomatic veils, providing an unparalleled insight into the enigmatic realm where nations, cultures, and ideologies converge in the pursuit of strategic advantage.

This book is an invitation to become astute observers of the silent dance that shapes our world, a call to recognize the forces at play beneath the surface, and an opportunity to comprehend the complex symphony of global affairs. Welcome to the world of silent diplomacy, where the silent handshake echoes louder than the spoken word, and hidden forces quietly mold the destiny of nations.

CHAPTER 1: THE UNSEEN CHESSBOARD: GEOPOLITICS UNVEILED

Geopolitics, often likened to a complex chess game played on the global stage, is a multifaceted arena where nations strategically maneuver their pieces in pursuit of power, influence, and national interests. This metaphorical chessboard extends far beyond the tangible realms of military might and economic prowess, delving into the intricate realms of diplomacy, ideology, and cultural exchange. The "Unseen Chessboard" encapsulates the clandestine and often obscured aspects of this geopolitical game, shedding light on the intricate maneuvers that shape the course of global affairs.

1. The Players and their Pieces: At the heart of the geopolitical chessboard are nations, each functioning as a player with its unique set of pieces. These pieces go beyond traditional military forces and encompass economic alliances, intelligence agencies, technological advancements, and even soft power initiatives such as cultural diplomacy and educational exchanges. The game involves a delicate balance of power, with each player striving to maximize its influence while minimizing vulnerabilities.

2. The Strategic Moves: Geopolitical maneuvering involves a series of strategic moves, akin to the opening, middle game, and endgame phases in chess. In the opening, nations establish alliances, build economic partnerships, and project military strength to secure advantageous positions. The middle game sees the players engaging in diplomatic negotiations, ideological battles, and economic competitions. The endgame, often marked by intense rivalries and power struggles, determines the ultimate winners and losers on the geopolitical chessboard.

3. The Role of Ideology and Culture: Ideological clashes and cultural influences serve as critical elements on the unseen chessboard. Nations project their values and beliefs, aiming to shape global narratives and garner support for their causes. Soft power becomes a potent tool, with cultural exports, educational initiatives, and media influencing the perceptions of other players and global audiences. The interplay between ideologies and cultures creates a dynamic landscape, where alliances are forged or broken based on shared values or conflicting beliefs.

4. Technological Advancements and Information Warfare: In the 21st century, the chessboard has evolved to incorporate technological advancements and information warfare. Cyber capabilities, artificial intelligence, and space exploration have become key battlegrounds. The ability to control and manipulate information, conduct cyber-espionage, and harness cutting-edge technologies provides players with unprecedented tools to gain an upper hand. The unseen maneuvers in the digital realm can reshape the geopolitical landscape without a single physical move.

5. The Geoeconomic Chessboard: Geoeconomics, the intersection of economic and geopolitical strategies, introduces a new dimension to the unseen chessboard. Trade wars, economic sanctions, and the quest for resource dominance become integral elements of the game. Nations strategically deploy economic instruments to coerce or entice their counterparts, leveraging economic interdependence as both a weapon and a shield. The global economy becomes a battlefield where economic prowess is a key determinant of geopolitical influence.

6. The Specter of Unconventional Warfare: Beyond traditional military engagements, the unseen chessboard witnesses the emergence of unconventional warfare. Proxy conflicts, asymmetric strategies, and hybrid warfare blur the lines between peace and conflict. Non-state actors and transnational forces play pivotal roles, introducing an element of unpredictability that challenges conventional notions of power dynamics.

7. The Unseen Players: In addition to nation-states, non-state actors, multinational corporations, and international organizations become influential players on the unseen chessboard. Non-governmental entities, with their global reach and resources, can shape narratives, influence policies, and impact geopolitical outcomes. The interconnectedness of the modern world ensures that the actions of a single player can send ripples across the entire chessboard.

8. The Great Game of the Future: As the geopolitical chessboard continues to evolve, the future promises new challenges and opportunities. Emerging technologies, environmental concerns, and shifting demographic landscapes will introduce additional variables to the game. The players must adapt their strategies to navigate these uncharted territories, ensuring that the unseen chessboard remains a dynamic and ever-changing arena.

In conclusion, the concept of the unseen chessboard in geopolitics encapsulates the intricate and often covert maneuvers that shape the global landscape. Beyond the overt displays of military might and economic strength, the game involves a complex interplay of ideologies, cultures, technologies, and economic strategies. Understanding this unseen dimension is crucial for deciphering the motivations and actions of nations on the world stage, as they engage in a perpetual game of strategy, influence, and power.

CHAPTER 2: SHADOWS OF POWER: UNDERSTANDING SILENT DIPLOMACY

Diplomacy, often perceived as the art of negotiation and dialogue between nations, encompasses a spectrum far broader than the publicized meetings and official statements that grace the headlines. Within the intricate fabric of international relations lies a clandestine realm known as silent diplomacy or, in a metaphorical sense, the "Shadows of Power." This nuanced and often covert aspect of diplomacy involves subtle, behind-the-scenes maneuvers that shape global affairs, yielding profound consequences on the geopolitical stage.

1. The Nature of Silent Diplomacy: Silent diplomacy thrives in the discreet exchanges, covert negotiations, and confidential agreements that occur away from the public eye. It operates in the shadows, beyond the scrutiny of media and public opinion, allowing nations to engage in delicate and often sensitive discussions without the constraints of public scrutiny.

2. Backchannel Communications: Backchannel communications serve as a cornerstone of silent diplomacy. These off-the-record dialogues occur through unofficial channels, enabling nations to explore ideas, test waters, and lay the groundwork for official negotiations. Such discreet channels can involve intelligence agencies, trusted intermediaries, or even informal gatherings where diplomats can speak candidly without the fear of immediate public backlash.

3. Track II Diplomacy: Track II diplomacy, another facet of silent diplomacy, involves non-governmental actors such as think tanks, academics, and private individuals. These unofficial channels provide a platform for open dialogue, fostering a more relaxed and exploratory environment. While not binding, the outcomes of Track II diplomacy can significantly influence official negotiations and contribute to building trust between nations.

4. Economic Leverage and Covert Alliances: Silent diplomacy extends into economic realms, where nations may use economic leverage as a tool to achieve diplomatic objectives. Covert alliances, often born out of shared economic interests, enable nations to collaborate discreetly, forming partnerships that may not be apparent on the surface. Economic incentives, trade agreements, and investment strategies become instruments in the silent diplomat's toolkit.

5. Intelligence and Covert Operations: The world of silent diplomacy intersects with intelligence operations, where information is a currency of immense value. Espionage, covert intelligence gathering, and cyber operations are all integral components of silent diplomacy. The information gleaned through these operations provides nations with insights into the strategies and vulnerabilities of their counterparts, shaping their diplomatic moves accordingly.

6. Crisis Management and Conflict Resolution: Silent diplomacy plays a crucial role in crisis management and conflict resolution. Behind closed doors, diplomats engage in shuttle diplomacy, shuttling between conflicting parties to explore potential resolutions. These quiet efforts aim to de-escalate tensions and find common ground, often preceding or running parallel to official peace talks.

7. Multilateral Forums and Informal Summits: Multilateral forums and informal summits provide platforms for silent diplomacy on a grand scale. Leaders may engage in private discussions during international conferences, allowing for candid conversations that go beyond scripted statements. These encounters contribute to building personal relationships, fostering mutual understanding, and laying the groundwork for future diplomatic endeavors.

8. The Role of Personal Envoys: Personal envoys, trusted individuals appointed by leaders to carry out discreet diplomatic missions, play a pivotal role in silent diplomacy. These envoys, possessing a deep understanding of the leader's intentions and preferences, can navigate complex negotiations with a degree of flexibility that official representatives might not have.

9. Cultural and Psychological Dimensions: Silent diplomacy recognizes the importance of cultural and psychological dimensions in international relations. Understanding the nuances of a nation's history, cultural sensitivities, and the psychological makeup of its leaders becomes essential in shaping effective silent diplomatic strategies.

10. The Risks and Ethical Dilemmas: While silent diplomacy can yield positive outcomes, it is not without risks and ethical dilemmas. The lack of transparency raises concerns about accountability, and covert actions may undermine democratic principles. Striking a balance between the need for discretion and the imperative of transparency remains a perennial challenge.

11. Technological Advances and Silent Warfare: In the modern era, technological advances introduce a new dimension to silent diplomacy. Cyber warfare, disinformation campaigns, and the weaponization of information amplify the impact of silent diplomacy. Navigating this landscape requires a keen understanding of the digital realm and the ability to counter or exploit these technologies for diplomatic ends.

12. The Future of Silent Diplomacy: As the global landscape continues to evolve, the future of silent diplomacy will be shaped by emerging challenges such as climate change, pandemics, and the ethical implications of technological advancements. The need for effective silent diplomacy becomes even more pronounced as nations grapple with increasingly complex and interconnected issues.

In conclusion, understanding the shadows of power in silent diplomacy is essential for comprehending the intricate dance of nations on the international stage. Beyond the overt displays of diplomacy lies a realm of discreet negotiations, covert operations, and subtle influences that shape the course of global affairs. Acknowledging the existence and impact of silent diplomacy is crucial for those seeking a comprehensive grasp of the complexities inherent in international relations.

CHAPTER 3: WHISPERS IN THE CORRIDORS: THE SUBTLE LANGUAGE OF INFLUENCE

In the intricate tapestry of power dynamics, there exists a realm where influence is wielded with finesse, a subtle dance in the shadows known as "Whispers in the Corridors." This metaphorical expression encapsulates the art of subtle influence, where unspoken cues, discreet conversations, and nuanced gestures shape the trajectory of decision-making in realms as diverse as politics, business, and interpersonal relationships. Understanding this subtle language is paramount for those navigating the corridors of power, where spoken words often carry less weight than the unspoken signals that permeate the air.

1. The Nature of Subtle Influence: Whispers in the corridors denote a form of influence that operates beneath the surface, manifesting in the unspoken exchanges that occur away from public scrutiny. This subtle language is characterized by its discretion, relying on the power of suggestion, body language, and carefully chosen words to convey messages without overt declarations.

2. Nonverbal Communication: A significant component of whispers in the corridors lies in nonverbal communication. The way individuals carry themselves, their gestures, facial expressions, and even their choice of attire can convey volumes without a single spoken word. Subtle cues such as a raised eyebrow, a nod of agreement, or a well-timed pause can carry profound implications in the language of influence.

3. The Power of Silence: Silence, often overlooked in a world dominated by vocal expression, is a potent tool in the corridors of power. The strategic use of silence can create a sense of anticipation, prompt introspection, or convey disapproval without the need for explicit verbalization. It becomes a canvas on which individuals paint unspoken messages.

4. Informal Networks and Cliques: Whispers in the corridors thrive within informal networks and cliques, where relationships are cultivated outside the formal structures of organizations or societies. These networks often transcend official hierarchies, allowing for the exchange of information, favors, and influence in ways that may not be apparent to those outside the inner circle.

5. Rumors and Controlled Leaks: The controlled dissemination of information, often in the form of rumors or strategically placed leaks, constitutes a powerful tool in the subtle language of influence. By carefully crafting narratives that may or may not be entirely accurate, individuals can shape perceptions, manipulate opinions, and advance their agendas without directly exposing their intentions.

6. Strategic Alliances and Coalitions: Whispers in the corridors facilitate the formation of strategic alliances and coalitions. Behind closed doors, individuals and entities align their interests, leveraging collective influence to achieve shared objectives. These alliances may not be explicitly stated but can significantly impact decision-making processes.

7. Lobbying and Advocacy: In political and corporate spheres, lobbying and advocacy serve as manifestations of whispers in the corridors. By engaging decision-makers in informal settings, lobbyists and advocates can subtly sway opinions, present perspectives, and influence policies without the overt confrontations associated with public discourse.

8. The Art of Indirect Communication: Whispers in the corridors rely on the art of indirect communication. Rather than expressing desires or intentions explicitly, influential individuals may convey their messages through anecdotes, metaphors, or hypothetical scenarios. This indirect approach allows for a degree of plausible deniability while still exerting influence.

9. Personal Relationships and Patronage: The cultivation of personal relationships and patronage relationships is a fundamental aspect of whispers in the corridors. Favors granted, mentorship provided, or allegiances formed in private can translate into significant influence when decisions are being made.

10. Adaptive Strategies in Different Cultures: The subtle language of influence varies across cultures, requiring individuals to adapt their strategies accordingly. In some cultures, indirect communication may be highly valued, while in others, directness may be more appreciated. Understanding the cultural nuances of whispers in the corridors is crucial for navigating diverse international arenas.

11. Managing Perception: Whispers in the corridors play a pivotal role in managing perception. Crafting a favorable image, influencing public opinion, and shaping the narrative around individuals or entities involve a delicate dance of whispers that permeate through various channels of communication.

12. Ethical Considerations: The use of whispers in the corridors raises ethical considerations. The discreet nature of this influence can border on manipulation, and the fine line between ethical persuasion and covert manipulation requires careful navigation. Striking a balance between ethical influence and the pursuit of objectives remains a perpetual challenge.

13. The Intersection with Technology: In the contemporary era, whispers in the corridors have extended into the digital realm. Social media, encrypted messaging platforms, and virtual spaces provide new avenues for subtle influence. Understanding the dynamics of online whispers becomes essential for those seeking to navigate the evolving landscape of power dynamics.

14. The Legacy of Whispers: The repercussions of whispers in the corridors may reverberate long after the initial exchanges. Decisions made, alliances formed, and narratives crafted through subtle influence can leave a lasting legacy, shaping the trajectory of institutions, societies, and even nations.

15. Navigating the Complex Web: Successfully navigating the complex web of whispers in the corridors requires a nuanced understanding of human psychology, cultural dynamics, and the intricacies of power structures. Individuals' adept at decoding the subtle language of influence can strategically position themselves to navigate the corridors of power effectively.

In conclusion, whispers in the corridors represent a sophisticated and often unspoken dimension of influence that permeates the fabric of society. Understanding this subtle language requires a keen awareness of nonverbal cues, cultural nuances, and the strategic use of information. Those proficient in the art of whispers in the corridors hold a key to unlocking doors of influence and shaping the course of events in ways that may not always be immediately apparent to the casual observer.

CHAPTER 4: BEYOND BORDERS: MAPPING GEOPOLITICAL TERRAIN

Geopolitics, the study of the interaction between geography, power, and politics, transcends national boundaries and operates in a global arena where strategic interests, alliances, and conflicts shape the course of international relations. The concept of "Beyond Borders" encapsulates the multifaceted nature of geopolitics, highlighting the complex interplay of factors that influence the geopolitical terrain on a global scale.

1. The Global Chessboard: Geopolitics unfolds on a vast global chessboard where nations are the players, and the pieces extend beyond traditional military forces. Economic strength, technological prowess, cultural influence, and diplomatic acumen all form integral components of this geopolitical chessboard. Understanding the nuances of this multifaceted game requires mapping the geopolitical terrain beyond the confines of national borders.

2. Strategic Resources and Geoeconomics: Beyond borders, nations vie for control over strategic resources that transcend their territorial limits. Energy, rare minerals, and water sources become focal points of geopolitical competition. Geoeconomics, the use of economic instruments for geopolitical purposes, emerges as a critical strategy where nations leverage their economic strength to gain influence and maneuver strategically on the global stage.

3. Regional Dynamics: Mapping geopolitical terrain involves a nuanced understanding of regional dynamics. Regional blocs, alliances, and conflicts shape the geopolitical landscape, influencing global power balances. The intricate relationships between neighboring nations, historical animosities, and regional organizations all contribute to the complexity of geopolitical dynamics beyond individual borders.

4. Transnational Threats: Beyond borders lie transnational threats that defy traditional notions of sovereignty. Issues such as climate change, pandemics, terrorism, and cyber threats permeate national boundaries, requiring international cooperation and coordinated strategies. Mapping the geopolitical terrain involves recognizing the shared challenges that necessitate collaborative responses.

5. Soft Power and Cultural Diplomacy: Geopolitics extends into the realm of soft power, where nations project influence through cultural diplomacy, education, and the export of ideas. Beyond military strength, a nation's cultural appeal and the attractiveness of its societal values contribute to shaping perceptions and alliances on the global stage.

6. Technological Frontiers: The rapid evolution of technology has expanded the geopolitical terrain into the digital realm. Cybersecurity, artificial intelligence, and space exploration become critical frontiers where nations seek dominance and influence. Mapping this technological landscape involves understanding the implications of digital advancements on global power structures.

7. International Institutions: Beyond national borders, international institutions play a pivotal role in shaping geopolitical dynamics. Organizations such as the United Nations, World Trade Organization, and regional bodies act as forums for diplomacy, conflict resolution, and economic cooperation. Navigating the geopolitical terrain requires an awareness of the strengths and limitations of these institutions.

8. Migration and Demographic Shifts: Demographic shifts and migration patterns contribute to the evolving geopolitical landscape. The movement of people across borders can influence cultural dynamics, economic systems, and even political landscapes. Mapping this aspect of geopolitics involves understanding the social and political consequences of demographic changes.

9. Maritime Geopolitics: Oceans and seas are crucial arenas in the mapping of geopolitical terrain. Maritime geopolitics involves the strategic control of sea routes, access to resources in exclusive economic zones, and the projection of naval power. The geopolitics of the seas transcends national borders, with implications for global trade and security.

10. Energy Security and Geostrategic Pipelines: Beyond borders, energy security becomes a critical geopolitical consideration. Nations engage in strategic partnerships and rivalries to secure access to energy resources, and the geopolitical terrain is shaped by the construction of pipelines and the control of key energy routes. Understanding the geopolitics of energy involves mapping the intricate network of pipelines and trade routes.

11. Economic Interdependence and Globalization: Economic interdependence, facilitated by globalization, creates a web of connections that transcends borders. The geopolitical terrain is influenced by economic ties, trade relationships, and investment flows. Navigating this interconnected landscape requires an understanding of how economic decisions in one part of the world can reverberate globally.

12. Environmental Geopolitics: Beyond borders, environmental concerns intersect with geopolitics. Climate change, resource depletion, and environmental degradation are geopolitical challenges that require international cooperation. Mapping the environmental geopolitics involves recognizing the shared responsibility of nations in addressing global environmental issues.

13. Military Alliances and Strategic Partnerships: Geopolitics involves the formation of military alliances and strategic partnerships that extend beyond individual borders. NATO, the Shanghai Cooperation Organization, and other regional defense pacts shape the security landscape on a global scale. Mapping these alliances is crucial for understanding the geopolitical balance of power.

14. Ideological Battlegrounds: Beyond borders, nations engage in ideological battles that influence geopolitical dynamics. Ideological clashes, driven by political systems, governance models, and value systems, contribute to the complexities of international relations. Mapping the ideological terrain involves recognizing the sources of tension and cooperation rooted in differing worldviews.

15. Geopolitics in Outer Space: The mapping of geopolitical terrain extends beyond Earth into outer space. The exploration and utilization of space resources, satellite technology, and space militarization introduce a new dimension to geopolitics. Nations vie for supremacy in the cosmic domain, shaping the rules and norms of space governance.

16. The Role of Non-State Actors: Geopolitical terrain is not solely defined by nation-states. Non-state actors such as multinational corporations, non-governmental organizations, and transnational groups wield significant influence. Understanding the role of these actors in shaping global affairs is integral to mapping the complete geopolitical landscape.

17. Unconventional Warfare and Asymmetric Threats: Beyond traditional military engagements, unconventional warfare and asymmetric threats pose challenges that extend beyond borders. Cyber warfare, hybrid tactics, and non-state actors create a dynamic geopolitical terrain that requires adaptive strategies and responses.

18. The Future of Geopolitical Mapping: The future of geopolitical mapping is shaped by emerging challenges such as technological advancements, climate change, and geopolitical realignments. The ability to anticipate and navigate the evolving terrain requires a forward-looking approach that integrates historical context, current trends, and future scenarios.

In conclusion, the concept of "Beyond Borders: Mapping

Geopolitical Terrain" underscores the intricate and interconnected nature of international relations. Geopolitics, as a multidimensional chessboard, extends beyond national boundaries, encompassing economic, technological, cultural, and environmental factors. Navigating this complex terrain requires a comprehensive understanding of the forces at play and the ability to adapt to the ever-changing dynamics of global affairs.

CHAPTER 5: THE SILENT HANDSHAKE: COVERT ALLIANCES IN GLOBAL POLITICS

In the realm of global politics, where alliances and partnerships often play a decisive role, the concept of the "Silent Handshake" emerges as a metaphor for covert alliances and discreet collaborations that operate beneath the surface of official diplomatic engagements. These clandestine partnerships, hidden from public view, wield significant influence and shape the geopolitical landscape in ways that extend beyond the overt alliances and treaties. Understanding the intricacies of the silent handshake is to unravel a covert dimension of international relations, where strategic interests and shared objectives give rise to partnerships that thrive in the shadows.

1. Covert Alliances Defined: Covert alliances, represented by the silent handshake, refer to discreet partnerships formed between nations or non-state actors with shared interests. Unlike traditional alliances that are openly declared and documented, covert alliances operate behind closed doors, often involving secret agreements, intelligence sharing, and collaborative strategies that remain hidden from public scrutiny.

2. Historical Precedents: Throughout history, covert alliances have played a pivotal role in shaping global politics. During World War II, for instance, the Allied forces engaged in covert collaborations with resistance movements, intelligence agencies, and non-state actors to counter Axis powers. The Cold War era also witnessed numerous covert alliances as superpowers sought to advance their interests without direct confrontation.

3. Intelligence Cooperation: The silent handshake often

involves intelligence cooperation, where nations share sensitive information and collaborate on covert operations. The exchange of intelligence enables partners to enhance their situational awareness, counter common threats, and manipulate geopolitical events in their favor. Such alliances may extend beyond traditional allies, involving unexpected or seemingly adversarial partnerships.

4. Proxy Wars and Covert Operations: Covert alliances frequently manifest in proxy wars and covert operations. Nations may support proxy groups or engage in clandestine activities to advance shared objectives without direct involvement. The silent handshake allows states to pursue their interests through plausible deniability, masking their true involvement in conflicts.

5. Economic Collaboration: Economic interests often drive covert alliances, with nations forming discreet partnerships to advance their economic agendas. This may involve joint ventures, trade agreements, and coordinated economic strategies that align with the partners' mutual goals. Economic collaboration through the silent handshake allows nations to exploit synergies without attracting unwanted attention.

6. Technological Collaborations: In an era where technological prowess is a key determinant of power, covert alliances extend into the realm of technology. Nations may engage in silent handshakes to share research and development efforts, pool resources for technological advancements, or collectively counter emerging threats in cyberspace and outer space.

7. Cultural and Ideological Alignments: Shared cultural and ideological affinities can form the basis for covert alliances. Nations with similar values and beliefs may engage in silent handshakes to promote their cultural influence, shape international narratives, and counter the influence of rivals. Soft power initiatives, cultural exchanges, and joint propaganda efforts may be part of these covert collaborations.

8. Nuclear Cooperation: Nuclear capabilities and proliferation present a unique arena for covert alliances. Nations seeking to enhance or maintain nuclear capabilities may engage in silent handshakes to acquire technology, materials, or expertise. Covert nuclear collaborations have the potential to disrupt the global balance of power and escalate regional tensions.

9. Strategic Maneuvering in International Organizations: Covert alliances extend into international organizations where states strategically maneuver to achieve their objectives. Voting blocs, lobbying efforts, and behind-the-scenes negotiations within organizations like the United Nations showcase the influence of the silent handshake in shaping resolutions, policies, and international norms.

10. Multinational Corporations and Covert Alliances: The silent handshake involves not only states but also multinational corporations that operate across borders. Covert collaborations between corporations and governments may occur to advance economic interests, shape regulatory environments, or gain a competitive edge in global markets. These alliances blur the lines between state and corporate interests.

11. Regional Hegemony and Power Brokers: Silent handshakes contribute to regional hegemony, with powerful states forming covert alliances to assert influence over neighboring regions. Power brokers emerge, manipulating regional dynamics through covert collaborations to ensure stability, counterbalance rivals, or advance economic interests.

12. Unconventional Partnerships: Covert alliances often involve unconventional partnerships that transcend traditional geopolitical alignments. States may form alliances with non-state actors, rebel groups, or factions within other nations to achieve shared objectives. These unconventional partnerships demonstrate the flexibility and adaptability of the silent handshake.

13. The Ethics and Dilemmas: Covert alliances raise ethical dilemmas and questions about transparency in international relations. The secrecy inherent in silent handshakes can undermine democratic principles, accountability, and the rule of law. Balancing the need for secrecy with the ethical considerations of covert collaborations remains a perpetual challenge.

14. The Role of Non-State Actors: Non-state actors, including intelligence agencies, private military contractors, and transnational organizations, often play a significant role in covert alliances. The silent handshake extends beyond the state level, with non-state actors contributing to the complexity and fluidity of these clandestine partnerships.

15. The Impact on Global Security: The silent handshake has a profound impact on global security. Covert alliances can either contribute to stability by preventing conflicts or exacerbate tensions by fueling proxy wars and geopolitical rivalries. Understanding the delicate balance between covert collaborations and global security is essential for policymakers and analysts.

16. The Future of Covert Alliances: As the geopolitical landscape continues to evolve, the future of covert alliances remains uncertain. Emerging technologies, environmental challenges, and shifting power dynamics will likely influence the nature and scope of silent handshakes. Adapting to these changes requires a keen understanding of the evolving geopolitical terrain.

In conclusion, the silent handshake represents a shadowy dimension of global politics, where covert alliances shape the course of international relations. Understanding these clandestine partnerships involves unraveling the complexities of intelligence cooperation, proxy conflicts, economic collaborations, and the multifaceted nature of global influence. Navigating the silent handshake requires diplomats, analysts, and policymakers to operate with a nuanced understanding

of the delicate dance occurring beneath the surface of official
diplomatic interactions.

CHAPTER 6: VEILED AGENDAS: DECODING STRATEGIC INTENTIONS

In the intricate landscape of international relations, strategic intentions often lie beneath the surface, shrouded in complexity and obscured by diplomatic rhetoric. The concept of "Veiled Agendas" delves into the art of decoding these strategic intentions, unraveling the hidden motives and objectives that guide the actions of nations on the global stage. This exploration encompasses the multifaceted dimensions of diplomatic maneuvers, military posturing, economic strategies, and covert operations, shedding light on the nuanced process of understanding the veiled agendas that shape the course of international affairs.

1. **The Nature of Veiled Agendas:** Veiled agendas are characterized by the deliberate concealment of true intentions behind a façade of diplomatic language, public posturing, and strategic ambiguity. Nations employ this tactic to safeguard sensitive information, manipulate perceptions, and maintain a degree of flexibility in their actions. Decoding veiled agendas requires a keen understanding of historical context, cultural nuances, and the geopolitical chessboard.

2. **Diplomatic Maneuvers:** Diplomacy serves as a primary arena for veiled agendas, where nations engage in intricate maneuvers to advance their interests without revealing their true intentions. Public statements, official communiqués, and diplomatic gestures often mask the underlying motives behind diplomatic actions. Analysts must decipher the language of diplomacy to unveil the strategic intentions beneath the surface.

3. **Military Posturing and Strategic Signaling:** Military

posturing is a tool through which veiled agendas manifest. Nations strategically deploy their armed forces, conduct joint exercises, or develop military capabilities to signal intentions without explicitly stating them. Understanding the subtleties of strategic signaling is essential for decoding the veiled agendas that influence the balance of power.

4. Economic Strategies: Economic maneuvers contribute significantly to veiled agendas. Nations may employ economic strategies such as trade policies, sanctions, and investment decisions to advance geopolitical objectives. Decoding these economic maneuvers involves analyzing the underlying political motives and discerning the intended impact on global and regional dynamics.

5. Covert Operations and Intelligence Activities: Veiled agendas often find expression in covert operations and intelligence activities. Espionage, cyber warfare, and covert interventions enable nations to pursue objectives discreetly. Deciphering the clues left by covert operations requires a deep understanding of the intelligence landscape and the ability to connect seemingly unrelated events.

6. Multilateral Diplomacy and Alliances: Multilateral diplomacy and alliance-building are arenas where veiled agendas are both crafted and deciphered. Nations form alliances to achieve common goals, but the true intentions behind these partnerships may not always be apparent. Analysts must navigate the complexities of multilateral interactions to unveil the strategic underpinnings of alliances.

7. Information Warfare and Propaganda: In the age of information, veiled agendas extend into the realm of information warfare and propaganda. Disinformation campaigns, manipulation of narratives, and the use of media as a tool for strategic influence all contribute to the complexities of decoding intentions. Analyzing the information landscape becomes crucial for understanding veiled agendas in the contemporary geopolitical arena.

8. Nuclear Diplomacy and Arms Control: Nuclear diplomacy involves veiled agendas centered on arms control, disarmament, and non-proliferation. Nations engage in negotiations and treaties to address nuclear issues, but the true motivations may involve broader strategic considerations. Decoding veiled agendas in nuclear diplomacy requires a nuanced understanding of the geopolitics surrounding nuclear capabilities.

9. Proxy Conflicts and Asymmetric Warfare: Veiled agendas often manifest in proxy conflicts and asymmetric warfare, where nations support surrogate groups or engage in unconventional tactics to achieve strategic goals. Decoding the motivations behind proxy conflicts involves analyzing the broader geopolitical context and identifying the hidden hands guiding these operations.

10. Geopolitical Grand Strategy: At the core of veiled agendas lies geopolitical grand strategy—a comprehensive vision that guides a nation's actions on the global stage. Decoding this grand strategy involves understanding the hierarchy of priorities, long-term objectives, and the calculus that shapes a nation's geopolitical decisions.

11. Technological Advancements: Technological advancements, especially in areas like artificial intelligence, cyber capabilities, and space exploration, introduce new dimensions to veiled agendas. Nations may pursue technological supremacy with strategic intentions that extend beyond the visible realm. Deciphering these technological strategies requires expertise in emerging technologies and their geopolitical implications.

12. Environmental and Resource Diplomacy: In the pursuit of environmental sustainability and resource security, nations engage in veiled agendas to secure access to critical resources and address global challenges. Decoding environmental and resource diplomacy involves unraveling the underlying geopolitical motivations behind international agreements, resource extraction, and conservation efforts.

13. Cultural Diplomacy and Soft Power: Soft power and cultural diplomacy contribute to veiled agendas as nations project a positive image to influence global perceptions. Decoding the cultural dimensions of veiled agendas requires an understanding of how nations use language, arts, and cultural exchanges to shape international narratives and gain influence.

14. The Role of Non-State Actors: Veiled agendas are not limited to states; non-state actors such as multinational corporations, non-governmental organizations, and transnational groups may also play a significant role. Deciphering the influence of non-state actors in global affairs requires an analysis of their relationships, motivations, and impact on geopolitical dynamics.

15. The Ethics of Decoding Veiled Agendas: The ethical dimensions of decoding veiled agendas raise questions about transparency, accountability, and the potential consequences of revealing hidden intentions. Striking a balance between the imperative of transparency and the need for strategic discretion remains a complex ethical challenge.

16. Global Governance and International Institutions: Veiled agendas intersect with global governance and international institutions. Nations may pursue hidden objectives within the framework of international organizations, shaping policies and decisions to align with their strategic goals. Decoding veiled agendas in global governance requires an understanding of the power dynamics within these institutions.

17. Unconventional Alliances and Shifting Alliances: Veiled agendas often lead to unconventional alliances and shifting allegiances as nations adapt to evolving geopolitical dynamics. Decoding the motives behind these alliances involves tracking changes in geopolitical interests, power dynamics, and emerging threats.

18. Navigating the Unseen Terrain: Decoding veiled agendas is a complex endeavor that requires a multidisciplinary approach. Analysts must synthesize information from diverse sources, interpret diplomatic signals, and discern patterns in seemingly unrelated events. Navigating the unseen terrain of veiled agendas demands a constant reassessment of geopolitical landscapes and an awareness of the evolving nature of global politics.

In conclusion, the world of veiled agendas is a realm of subtle complexities, strategic maneuvers, and hidden motivations that shape the international order. Decoding these agendas demands a nuanced understanding of the geopolitical chessboard, an ability to interpret signals, and an awareness of the multidimensional factors that influence the actions of nations on the global stage. As the world continues to evolve, the skill of decoding veiled agendas remains essential for those seeking to unravel the mysteries that lie beneath the surface of international relations.

CHAPTER 7: PROXY GAMES: GEOPOLITICAL CHESS IN THE MODERN ERA

In the complex theater of international relations, the term "Proxy Games" captures the strategic maneuvers and geopolitical chess played out indirectly through surrogate actors on behalf of major powers. This phenomenon has evolved and adapted to the dynamics of the modern era, where state and non-state actors engage in covert, unconventional, and often deniable tactics to advance their interests, extend influence, and achieve strategic goals without direct confrontation. Understanding the intricacies of Proxy Games requires delving into historical context, regional conflicts, shifting alliances, and the evolving tools of statecraft in the contemporary geopolitical landscape.

1. Historical Foundations: The roots of Proxy Games can be traced back to the Cold War, where the United States and the Soviet Union engaged in indirect conflicts to expand their spheres of influence without direct military confrontation. Examples include the Korean War, Vietnam War, and conflicts in Africa and Latin America, where proxy actors became pawns in the superpowers' ideological struggle.

2. Modern Geopolitical Context: In the modern era, Proxy Games persist but have taken on new dimensions. Regional powers, emerging nations, and non-state actors have joined the stage, creating a more multipolar and dynamic geopolitical environment. The Middle East, Eastern Europe, and parts of Asia have become hotbeds for contemporary Proxy Games, with major and regional powers vying for influence.

3. Proxy Actors and Non-State Entities: Proxy Games involve a diverse array of actors beyond traditional state entities. Non-state actors, including rebel groups, militias, and terrorist organizations, are often employed as proxies to advance the interests of sponsoring states. These proxies offer deniability to their sponsors, creating a layer of complexity in deciphering the true architects behind conflicts.

4. Ideological, Religious, and Ethnic Motivations: Proxy Games often leverage ideological, religious, or ethnic motivations to recruit and mobilize proxy actors. Sponsoring states may exploit existing fault lines within a region to fuel conflicts that align with their strategic objectives. The use of identity-based motivations adds a layer of complexity to Proxy Games, as it intertwines geopolitical interests with deeply rooted societal factors.

5. Cyber Proxy Games: The digital age has introduced a new dimension to Proxy Games through cyber warfare and information operations. States may engage in proxy conflicts by supporting or conducting cyber-attacks against adversaries. The use of hackers, disinformation campaigns, and cyber espionage serves as a covert tool for advancing strategic interests in the modern era.

6. Economic Proxy Dynamics: Economic leverage is a key facet of Proxy Games, with nations using economic incentives, sanctions, and trade as tools to influence the behavior of proxy actors or disrupt the economies of rival states. Economic pressure becomes a subtle yet powerful means to manipulate geopolitical outcomes without overt military engagement.

7. Regional Power Dynamics: Proxy Games are often embedded in regional power dynamics, with neighboring states or regional powers vying for influence. The conflicts in the Middle East, for example, see major powers supporting opposing proxy actors to secure strategic advantages and reshape the regional balance of power.

8. Energy Resources and Proxy Conflicts: Control over energy resources plays a central role in Proxy Games. Sponsoring states may support proxy actors in regions rich in oil and gas to secure access to vital resources and exert influence over global energy markets. The geopolitics of energy intertwine with proxy conflicts, creating complex and intertwined motivations.

9. Refugee Crisis as a Proxy Outcome: Proxy conflicts often lead to humanitarian crises, including mass displacements and refugee flows. The displacement of populations can be used as a tool in Proxy Games, destabilizing adversaries and placing economic, social, and political burdens on rival states and regions.

10. Hybrid Warfare: Proxy Games frequently involve hybrid warfare, a combination of conventional military tactics, irregular warfare, and information operations. Sponsoring states may employ a mix of military, economic, and informational tools to achieve their objectives through proxy actors while maintaining plausible deniability.

11. The Role of Arms Sales: Arms sales and military assistance serve as instruments in Proxy Games. States may supply weapons and military equipment to proxy actors, fueling conflicts and sustaining their influence. The global arms trade becomes intertwined with proxy conflicts, contributing to regional instability.

12. Proxy Games in the Arctic and Space: As geopolitical competition extends to new frontiers; Proxy Games are now observed in the Arctic and outer space. States compete indirectly for control over the Arctic's resources and strategic sea routes. In space, the militarization of satellites and space-based technologies adds a new dimension to Proxy Games in the quest for strategic dominance.

13. Intelligence and Covert Operations: Intelligence agencies play a crucial role in Proxy Games, conducting covert operations, gathering information, and influencing proxy actors. Espionage, covert funding, and the training of proxy forces contribute to the shadowy and deniable aspects of Proxy Games.

14. The Role of Ideological Alliances: Proxy Games often involve the creation of ideological alliances, where states with similar political or religious ideologies support proxy actors aligned with their worldview. This form of ideological collaboration deepens the complexities of proxy conflicts and aligns them with broader global ideological struggles.

15. Shifting Alliances and Unpredictability: Proxy Games are marked by the fluidity of alliances, with states switching allegiances based on shifting geopolitical realities. The unpredictability of proxy conflicts adds an element of volatility to international relations, making it challenging for analysts and policymakers to anticipate and respond effectively.

16. The Human Cost: Proxy Games exact a significant human cost, with civilians often caught in the crossfire of conflicts fueled by proxy actors. Humanitarian crises, displacement, and the destruction of infrastructure become consequences of proxy conflicts, underscoring the ethical dimensions and the toll on innocent lives.

17. International Responses and Mediation: The international community responds to Proxy Games through diplomatic efforts, sanctions, and peacekeeping initiatives. Mediation becomes a critical tool in resolving proxy conflicts and mitigating the broader geopolitical consequences. However, navigating the complexities of Proxy Games requires a delicate balance between national interests and global stability.

18. Navigating Proxy Games in the Future: As the geopolitical landscape evolves, the future of Proxy Games will be shaped by emerging technologies, environmental challenges, and shifts in global power dynamics. Policymakers and analysts must remain vigilant in navigating the complexities of Proxy Games to anticipate and respond to the ever-changing nature of indirect conflicts.

In conclusion, Proxy Games represent a pervasive and intricate dimension of modern geopolitics, where states and non-state actors engage in indirect conflicts to advance their strategic interests. The evolution of Proxy Games reflects the shifting dynamics of international relations, incorporating new tools, domains, and motivations. Deciphering the complexities of Proxy Games demands a comprehensive understanding of historical context, regional dynamics, and the multifaceted strategies employed by actors on the global stage.

CHAPTER 8: ECHOES OF HISTORY: THE PERSISTENT IMPACT ON GLOBAL DYNAMICS

History, often referred to as the master teacher, leaves an indelible mark on the tapestry of human civilization. The echoes of historical events reverberate through time, shaping the present and influencing the trajectory of global dynamics. This profound interplay between past and present is the essence of "Echoes of History," a concept that delves into the enduring impact of historical legacies, conflicts, cultural exchanges, and transformative moments on the complex stage of international relations. Understanding these echoes requires a journey through time, traversing diverse civilizations, conflicts, and cultural exchanges that have left an enduring imprint on the world's geopolitical landscape.

1. Historical Roots of Contemporary Conflicts: The origins of many contemporary conflicts can be traced back to historical grievances, territorial disputes, and power struggles. Echoes of colonialism, imperial ambitions, and the redrawing of borders during significant historical events continue to shape conflicts in regions such as the Middle East, South Asia, and Africa. Understanding the historical roots is crucial for grasping the complexities of these ongoing struggles.

2. Legacy of Imperialism and Colonialism: The legacy of imperialism and colonialism casts a long shadow on global dynamics. The artificial borders drawn by colonial powers, exploitation of resources, and cultural impositions have left lasting impacts on post-colonial societies. Economic disparities, ethnic tensions, and identity struggles in various regions can be traced back to the imperial era.

3. The World Wars and Shifting Power Dynamics: The two World Wars of the 20th century dramatically reshaped global power dynamics. The aftermath of World War I gave rise to the League of Nations, while World War II led to the establishment of the United Nations. The echoes of these conflicts are evident in the structures of international governance, the balance of power, and the pursuit of collective security.

4. Cold War Legacy: The Cold War between the United States and the Soviet Union had a profound impact on global dynamics. The ideological and geopolitical competition left a legacy of proxy conflicts, the division of nations into blocs, and the arms race. The remnants of Cold War rivalries still influence geopolitical alliances, regional tensions, and the nuclear landscape.

5. The Decolonization Wave: The mid-20th century witnessed a wave of decolonization as nations sought independence from colonial rule. The echoes of this movement resonate in the geopolitical realignment, regional conflicts, and struggles for self-determination that persist in various parts of the world today. The aftermath of decolonization continues to shape post-colonial identities and international relations.

6. Cultural Exchanges and the Silk Road: Historical cultural exchanges, exemplified by the Silk Road, have fostered connections between civilizations for centuries. The exchange of ideas, technologies, and goods along these ancient trade routes has left a cultural legacy that can be observed in today's global interconnectedness, with echoes of historical exchange shaping contemporary cultural diversity and understanding.

7. The Renaissance and the Age of Enlightenment: The Renaissance and the Age of Enlightenment marked transformative periods in history, fostering intellectual, artistic, and scientific advancements. The ideas of individual rights, reason, and liberty that emerged during these eras continue to influence political philosophies, governance structures, and human rights principles in the contemporary world.

8. Legacy of Genocides and Atrocities: The echoes of genocides and atrocities, such as the Holocaust and other instances of mass violence, linger as haunting reminders of humanity's capacity for cruelty. These historical traumas shape international efforts for justice, human rights advocacy, and the prevention of such horrors in the present day.

9. The Impact of Revolutions: Revolutions, from the French Revolution to the Russian Revolution, have transformed political landscapes and inspired movements for social change. The echoes of revolutionary ideals, including democracy, equality, and self-determination, resonate in contemporary struggles for political rights and social justice worldwide.

10. Economic Transformations and Industrialization: The Industrial Revolution and subsequent economic transformations have left an enduring impact on global economic dynamics. The shift from agrarian societies to industrial economies has shaped patterns of trade, technological innovation, and economic inequalities that persist in the modern era.

11. Technology and the Information Age: The rapid advancements in technology, particularly during the Information Age, have roots in historical breakthroughs. The echoes of the scientific revolution, the invention of the printing press, and the industrial innovations of the 19th century are evident in the digital revolution, telecommunications, and the interconnectedness of the contemporary world.

12. Environmental Consequences: Historical activities, including industrialization and colonial resource exploitation, have contributed to environmental challenges. The echoes of historical environmental degradation impact contemporary efforts to address climate change, deforestation, and sustainable development. Historical decisions and practices continue to influence the delicate balance between human activities and the planet.

13. Diplomacy and Treaties: Historical diplomatic agreements and treaties shape the foundations of modern international relations. Treaties like the Treaty of Westphalia and the Treaty of Versailles have set precedents for state sovereignty and the resolution of conflicts. The echoes of diplomatic engagements reverberate in contemporary efforts to establish international norms and cooperation.

14. Lessons from Pandemics and Health Crises: Historical pandemics, such as the Spanish flu, offer lessons that resonate in the response to modern health crises. The echoes of past experiences influence global efforts to address pandemics, emphasizing the importance of international cooperation, scientific research, and public health measures.

15. The Evolution of Democracy: The historical evolution of democratic ideals, from ancient Greece to the Enlightenment, has shaped the contemporary understanding of governance. Echoes of democratic principles influence political movements, institutions, and aspirations for self-determination in nations around the world.

16. Soft Power and Cultural Diplomacy: The use of soft power and cultural diplomacy has historical roots in the exchange of ideas, arts, and values between civilizations. Historical cultural exchanges, such as the Silk Road, contribute to the contemporary projection of soft power, where nations seek to influence others through cultural appeal, education, and information.

17. Lessons from Global Cooperation: Historical instances of successful global cooperation, such as the establishment of the United Nations after World War II, offer lessons for addressing contemporary challenges. The echoes of collaborative efforts shape modern endeavors to address transnational issues, including climate change, pandemics, and humanitarian crises.

18. Challenges of Historical Baggage: While history provides valuable lessons, it also presents challenges in the form of historical baggage, unresolved conflicts, and deep-seated animosities. The echoes of historical grievances can fuel ongoing tensions, hindering diplomatic resolutions and perpetuating cycles of violence.

In conclusion, the echoes of history resonate through the corridors of time, influencing global dynamics in profound and intricate ways. The persistent impact of historical events, cultural exchanges, and transformative moments is evident in the geopolitical, economic, and cultural tapestry of the modern era. Understanding these echoes is not merely a scholarly pursuit but a vital tool for policymakers, diplomats, and global citizens seeking to navigate the complexities of our interconnected world with wisdom drawn from the lessons of the past.

CHAPTER 9: SILENT ARCHITECTS: CRAFTING THE GEOPOLITICAL LANDSCAPE

In the intricate tapestry of international relations, the concept of "Silent Architects" refers to the often unseen and discreet actors who, through strategic decisions, covert maneuvers, and long-term planning, shape and craft the geopolitical landscape. These architects operate behind the scenes, orchestrating events, alliances, and structures that influence the balance of power on the global stage. To understand the role of Silent Architects is to unravel the complexities of their methods, motivations, and the lasting impact they have on the ever-evolving geopolitical landscape.

1. Covert Decision-Making and Strategic Calculations: Silent Architects are distinguished by their ability to make decisions covertly, away from the public eye. These decisions range from intelligence operations and covert interventions to economic strategies that influence the geopolitical landscape. The clandestine nature of their actions allows for strategic calculations that may not be possible in the open arena of international relations.

2. Intelligence Agencies and Covert Operations: Among the most prominent Silent Architects are intelligence agencies, which operate in the shadows to gather information, conduct covert operations, and influence events in favor of their sponsoring nations. The historical examples of intelligence agencies, such as the CIA and the KGB during the Cold War, showcase the significant impact Silent Architects can have on shaping global dynamics.

3. Economic Puppetry and Financial Instruments: Silent

Architects often leverage economic tools to craft the geopolitical landscape. Through financial instruments, trade agreements, and economic sanctions, they can manipulate the economic fortunes of nations. This economic puppetry not only influences individual countries but also contributes to the restructuring of global economic hierarchies.

4. Multilateral Organizations and Global Governance: Silent Architects extend their influence through multilateral organizations and global governance structures. By strategically positioning themselves within international institutions, they can shape policies, influence decision-making processes, and promote their own geopolitical agendas. The United Nations, World Bank, and International Monetary Fund are arenas where Silent Architects subtly exert their influence.

5. Non-Governmental Organizations (NGOs) and Soft Power: NGOs, ostensibly independent entities, are sometimes utilized as instruments of Silent Architects to exert soft power. By shaping narratives, influencing public opinion, and advocating for specific causes, these organizations contribute to crafting the geopolitical landscape. Their influence is subtle yet pervasive, impacting issues ranging from human rights to environmental policies.

6. Cultural Diplomacy and Information Warfare: Silent Architects recognize the power of cultural diplomacy and information warfare. Through the strategic dissemination of information, manipulation of narratives, and control over cultural exchanges, they shape perceptions and opinions on the global stage. Cultural influence becomes a tool for crafting a favorable geopolitical environment.

7. Technological Advancements and Cyber Warfare: In the digital age, Silent Architects leverage technological advancements and engage in cyber warfare to further their objectives. From hacking and information manipulation to the militarization of cyberspace, they exploit vulnerabilities in the digital realm to shape geopolitical outcomes.

8. Military Industrial Complex: The military-industrial complex, a term coined by President Dwight D. Eisenhower, is a manifestation of Silent Architects' influence. By fostering the interdependence of military and industrial interests, they ensure the perpetuation of military capabilities, influence defense policies, and contribute to the global arms race.

9. Proxy Conflicts and Unconventional Alliances: Silent Architects often operate through proxies, supporting unconventional alliances to achieve their goals indirectly. Proxy conflicts, where nations support surrogate actors in conflicts, are a hallmark of this approach. The use of non-state actors allows Silent Architects to maintain plausible deniability while influencing events.

10. Geoeconomic Strategies and Resource Control: Geoeconomic strategies involve the use of economic instruments to achieve geopolitical objectives. Silent Architects may exert control over critical resources, such as oil and minerals, shaping the economic fortunes of nations and influencing their geopolitical alignments.

11. Treaty Negotiations and Diplomatic Maneuvers: Behind treaty negotiations and diplomatic maneuvers, Silent Architects strategically position nations to advance their long-term interests. The negotiation of treaties, alliances, and diplomatic agreements becomes a subtle yet powerful tool for crafting the geopolitical landscape.

12. Regional Power Brokers and Hegemonic Ambitions: Silent Architects often operate at the regional level, aligning themselves with aspiring regional power brokers. By supporting nations with hegemonic ambitions, they contribute to regional dominance and influence the power dynamics within specific geographic areas.

13. Intelligence Alliances and Coordinated Efforts: Silent Architects excel in forming intelligence alliances and coordinating efforts among like-minded nations. These collaborations enhance their collective intelligence capabilities, enabling them to preemptively respond to emerging geopolitical challenges and opportunities.

14. Climate Diplomacy and Environmental Policies: With the growing importance of environmental issues, Silent Architects extend their influence into climate diplomacy and environmental policies. By shaping international agreements and environmental regulations, they craft the geopolitical landscape with an eye on sustainability, resource management, and global cooperation.

15. Nuclear Strategies and Arms Control: Silent Architects play a pivotal role in nuclear strategies and arms control negotiations. By influencing the development, deployment, and control of nuclear weapons, they contribute to the delicate balance of power and deterrence in global affairs.

16. Shaping Global Narratives and Perception Management: The control of global narratives is a potent tool in the arsenal of Silent Architects. Through perception management, they shape how events are interpreted and portrayed, influencing public opinion and the policies of nations.

17. Unseen Contributions of Non-State Actors: Silent Architects also engage non-state actors, including multinational corporations, think tanks, and influential individuals, to further their objectives. Non-state actors often operate beyond traditional diplomatic constraints, allowing Silent Architects to leverage their influence discreetly.

18. Ethical Considerations and Accountability: The actions of Silent Architects raise ethical considerations, as their covert maneuvers may undermine democratic principles, transparency, and accountability. Balancing the imperatives of strategic discretion with the ethical dimensions of their actions poses a perpetual challenge.

In conclusion, the Silent Architects wield an unseen influence over the geopolitical landscape, employing covert methods, strategic calculations, and long-term planning to shape the course of international relations. From intelligence agencies and economic instruments to cultural diplomacy and cyber warfare, their toolkit is diverse and adaptable. Recognizing the role of Silent Architects is essential for understanding the multifaceted nature of global dynamics and navigating the complexities of a world where much of the shaping occurs behind the scenes.

CHAPTER 10: UNDERCURRENTS OF CONFLICT: UNRAVELING HIDDEN TENSIONS

In the complex realm of international relations, the concept of "Undercurrents of Conflict" refers to the subtle and often concealed dynamics that contribute to tensions between nations. These hidden tensions, manifesting beneath the surface of diplomatic interactions and geopolitical posturing, shape the contours of global affairs. Understanding the undercurrents involves delving into historical grievances, identity politics, economic rivalries, and strategic considerations that may not be immediately evident. This exploration seeks to unravel the nuanced and multifaceted nature of hidden tensions that have the potential to erupt into open conflict and reshape the geopolitical landscape.

1. Historical Resentments and Unresolved Grievances: Undercurrents of conflict often find their roots in historical events, where unresolved grievances and resentments continue to simmer beneath the surface. Historical injustices, territorial disputes, and the lingering impact of past conflicts cast shadows that influence contemporary relations between nations.

2. Identity Politics and Nationalism: Identity politics, driven by nationalism and a sense of collective identity, contributes significantly to hidden tensions. Cultural, ethnic, and religious differences may be manipulated by political leaders to foster a sense of 'us versus them,' creating undercurrents of conflict that transcend traditional diplomatic channels.

3. Economic Rivalries and Resource Competition: Hidden tensions frequently emerge from economic rivalries and competition for vital resources. Control over strategic resources, trade routes, and economic dominance can become flashpoints for conflict, with nations jockeying for advantageous positions in the global economic order.

4. Proxy Conflicts and Covert Operations: Undercurrents of conflict extend into the realm of proxy conflicts and covert operations. Nations may engage in supporting proxy actors, conducting covert interventions, or employing asymmetric warfare to advance their interests without direct confrontation. Deciphering these hidden maneuvers is crucial for understanding the dynamics of global conflicts.

5. Ideological Clashes and Value Systems: Underlying ideological clashes and clashes of value systems contribute to hidden tensions. Differences in political ideologies, governance structures, and cultural norms can fuel undercurrents of conflict, creating fault lines that manifest in diplomatic standoffs and geopolitical rivalries.

6. Strategic Geopolitical Considerations: Nations often operate with long-term strategic considerations that may not be immediately visible. Undercurrents of conflict arise from geopolitical calculations, where nations position themselves strategically to counter perceived threats, expand influence, or safeguard their national interests.

7. Military Buildups and Arms Races: The buildup of military capabilities and the proliferation of arms contribute to hidden tensions. Nations engaging in arms races or rapidly expanding their military capabilities may trigger concerns among neighbors, setting the stage for undercurrents of conflict that reverberate through regional and global security landscapes.

8. Territorial Disputes and Border Issues: Territorial disputes and border issues are perennial sources of hidden tensions. Unresolved questions about borders, maritime boundaries, and territorial sovereignty can lead to diplomatic friction and, in extreme cases, result in open conflict if left unaddressed.

9. Regional Power Struggles: Hidden tensions often manifest in regional power struggles, with nations vying for dominance within their geographic spheres of influence. Regional power dynamics contribute to undercurrents of conflict as nations seek to assert their hegemony and shape the political landscape in their favor.

10. Human Rights and Ethical Dilemmas: Undercurrents of conflict may arise from concerns related to human rights abuses and ethical dilemmas. Nations grappling with internal repression or engaging in questionable practices may face international scrutiny, leading to hidden tensions as diplomatic pressure builds.

11. Unpredictable Leadership Dynamics: The unpredictability of leadership dynamics, characterized by shifts in leadership styles, ideologies, or policy directions, can contribute to hidden tensions. Sudden changes in leadership may alter the geopolitical calculus, creating uncertainties and triggering undercurrents of conflict.

12. Nuclear Proliferation and Arms Control: The pursuit of nuclear weapons and issues related to arms control contribute to hidden tensions. The strategic implications of nuclear proliferation, coupled with the complexities of arms control negotiations, create undercurrents that influence the global balance of power.

13. Cybersecurity Threats and Technological Competitions: In the digital age, hidden tensions arise from cybersecurity threats and technological competitions. Nations engaged in cyber warfare, espionage, and the race for technological supremacy contribute to undercurrents of conflict that extend into the realm of information and communication technologies.

14. Environmental Stewardship and Resource Scarcity: Environmental concerns and resource scarcity contribute to undercurrents of conflict as nations grapple with the impacts of climate change, depletion of natural resources, and competition for access to critical commodities. Environmental stewardship becomes intertwined with geopolitical considerations.

15. Regional Alliances and Shifting Allegiances: The formation of regional alliances and the shifting of allegiances contribute to hidden tensions. Nations strategically align themselves with like-minded partners, creating undercurrents of conflict as geopolitical blocs evolve and realign.

16. Competition for International Influence: Nations engage in subtle competitions for international influence, seeking to shape global narratives, garner support in international forums, and project soft power. The undercurrents of conflict in this arena involve diplomatic maneuvers, information warfare, and the strategic projection of national interests.

17. Influence of Non-State Actors: Non-state actors, including multinational corporations, influential individuals, and transnational organizations, can contribute to hidden tensions. The influence wielded by these entities in shaping economic policies, public opinion, and international agendas creates undercurrents that impact the traditional state-centric geopolitical landscape.

18. Challenges of Multilateral Diplomacy: Multilateral diplomacy, while essential for addressing global challenges, can also be a source of hidden tensions. Competing interests, divergent priorities, and the complexities of navigating international institutions contribute to undercurrents of conflict within the framework of global governance.

In conclusion, the undercurrents of conflict represent the complex and often concealed dynamics that shape the world of international relations. Understanding these hidden tensions requires a nuanced analysis of historical legacies, economic rivalries, strategic considerations, and the interplay of diverse factors that influence the geopolitical landscape. Navigating these undercurrents is a perpetual challenge for policymakers, diplomats, and global citizens seeking to foster stability, prevent conflicts, and build a more harmonious world.

CHAPTER 11: THE QUIET REVOLUTION: TECHNOLOGICAL FORCES IN GEOPOLITICS

The advent of the digital age has ushered in a transformative era, characterized by a silent yet profound revolution in the intersection of technology and geopolitics. The "Quiet Revolution" refers to the sweeping changes in global dynamics driven by technological forces, reshaping the geopolitical landscape in ways that extend beyond conventional power dynamics. Understanding this revolution entails exploring the multifaceted impact of technologies such as artificial intelligence, cyber capabilities, space exploration, biotechnology, and the Internet of Things (IoT) on the strategies, power structures, and interactions of nations in the contemporary world.

1. The Rise of Information Warfare: One of the pivotal aspects of the Quiet Revolution is the rise of information warfare. Nations harness the power of cyberspace to engage in covert operations, influence public opinion, and disrupt the systems of adversaries. Cyber-attacks, disinformation campaigns, and the weaponization of information have become key tools in the arsenal of states seeking to shape narratives and undermine the stability of rival nations.

2. Artificial Intelligence (AI) and Strategic Advantage: AI stands at the forefront of the Quiet Revolution, offering nations unprecedented capabilities in data analysis, predictive modeling, and decision-making. AI-driven technologies influence military strategies, economic planning, and intelligence gathering. The race for AI supremacy has become a significant determinant of geopolitical power, as nations seek a strategic advantage in the era of machine intelligence.

3. Space Exploration and Militarization: The quiet expanse of outer space has become a new frontier for geopolitical competition. Nations are increasingly investing in space exploration, satellite technologies, and space-based capabilities for communication, surveillance, and navigation. The militarization of space introduces a new dimension to geopolitical power, where control over orbital assets becomes a strategic imperative.

4. 5G Technology and Connectivity Dominance: The rollout of 5G technology represents a critical component of the Quiet Revolution. Nations vie for dominance in the race to implement 5G infrastructure, as it underpins the connectivity of the future. Control over 5G networks confers not only economic advantages but also the ability to shape global communication networks, influencing information flows and technological dependencies.

5. Biotechnology and the New Frontier of Power: Advances in biotechnology, including gene editing and synthetic biology, are redefining the contours of geopolitical power. Nations invest in biosecurity, health technologies, and biodefense capabilities. The ability to manipulate biological systems and harness biotechnological innovations introduces novel considerations for national security and global influence.

6. Internet of Things (IoT) and Smart Infrastructure: The proliferation of connected devices through the Internet of Things (IoT) transforms traditional notions of security. Smart infrastructure, including interconnected systems in energy, transportation, and healthcare, introduces new vulnerabilities. Nation's grapple with the challenges of securing critical IoT networks to prevent cyber threats and safeguard against potential disruptions.

7. Quantum Computing and Cryptography Challenges: Quantum computing poses both opportunities and challenges in the Quiet Revolution. While offering the potential for unprecedented computational power, it also threatens traditional cryptographic systems. Nations invest in quantum-resistant encryption and explore the strategic implications of quantum computing in fields such as cybersecurity and code-breaking.

8. Renewable Energy and Energy Security: The quest for renewable energy sources shapes geopolitical strategies in the Quiet Revolution. Nations seek energy security through investments in solar, wind, and other sustainable technologies. Control over energy resources, including the minerals essential for renewable technologies, becomes a factor in global power dynamics.

9. Technological Nationalism and Supply Chain Resilience: The Quiet Revolution witnesses the rise of technological nationalism, where nations assert control over critical technologies and supply chains. This shift is driven by concerns about supply chain vulnerabilities, economic dependencies, and the need to ensure resilience in the face of geopolitical uncertainties.

10. Surveillance Technologies and Privacy Concerns: Advances in surveillance technologies, including facial recognition, biometric identification, and mass data collection, raise profound ethical and privacy concerns. The integration of surveillance into statecraft influences the dynamics of governance, human rights, and international relations, adding a layer of complexity to geopolitical considerations.

11. Environmental Technologies and Climate Diplomacy: The Quiet Revolution extends to environmental technologies as nations grapple with the impacts of climate change. The development of green technologies, sustainable practices, and climate mitigation strategies becomes intertwined with geopolitical influence and diplomatic efforts to address shared environmental challenges.

12. Global Health Technologies and Pandemic Preparedness: Recent global events, such as the COVID-19 pandemic, underscore the role of health technologies in geopolitical considerations. Nations prioritize pandemic preparedness, vaccine development, and global health collaboration as part of their strategies to address health crises and secure their populations.

13. Tech Cold War and Geoeconomic Strategies: The Quiet Revolution has given rise to a new form of competition often referred to as the "Tech Cold War." Nations engage in geoeconomic strategies, using technology as a tool for influence, market dominance, and control over critical sectors. The race for technological supremacy shapes global economic alliances and rivalries.

14. Regulatory Challenges and International Norms: As technologies advance, regulatory challenges emerge. Nations grapple with establishing international norms and governance frameworks to address ethical considerations, cybersecurity threats, and the responsible use of emerging technologies. The absence of clear regulatory standards contributes to geopolitical uncertainties.

15. Cybersecurity Dilemmas and Hybrid Threats: The Quiet Revolution amplifies cybersecurity dilemmas as nations confront hybrid threats that blend conventional and cyber warfare tactics. The need for robust cybersecurity measures, international cooperation, and the development of cyber norms becomes imperative to mitigate the risks of conflict escalation in the digital realm.

16. Tech Diplomacy and Soft Power Projection: Nations increasingly leverage technology for diplomatic influence and soft power projection. Technological achievements, innovation ecosystems, and digital connectivity contribute to a nation's global image and influence. Tech diplomacy becomes a strategic tool for building alliances and shaping perceptions on the global stage.

17. Ethical Considerations and Technological Accountability:

The Quiet Revolution raises ethical considerations about the responsible use of technology. Nations grapple with issues of privacy, autonomy, and the unintended consequences of technological advancements. The pursuit of technological accountability becomes an integral aspect of ethical governance in the digital age.

18. The Human Factor and Technological Empowerment: Amid the technological shifts, the human factor remains central. The Quiet Revolution empowers individuals and civil society with unprecedented access to information, communication, and collaboration. The role of empowered citizens in shaping geopolitical narratives and influencing governance becomes a dynamic force in the evolving global landscape.

In conclusion, the Quiet Revolution driven by technological forces represents a paradigm shift in geopolitics. The intricate interplay of artificial intelligence, space exploration, biotechnology, connectivity, and other technological advancements reshapes the strategies and power dynamics of nations. Navigating this revolution requires a delicate balance between harnessing the benefits of technological progress and addressing the ethical, security, and governance challenges that arise in an interconnected world propelled by innovation. The geopolitical stage, silently transformed by these technological undercurrents, awaits the continued evolution of the Quiet Revolution in the years to come.

CHAPTER 12: COERCIVE DIPLOMACY: THE ART OF SILENT PRESSURE

In the intricate dance of international relations, where words are as significant as actions, the concept of "Coercive Diplomacy" emerges as a nuanced and strategic approach to achieving diplomatic objectives through the artful application of silent pressure. This diplomatic tactic involves the delicate orchestration of political, economic, and military instruments to influence the behavior of other nations without resorting to overt aggression. To understand the intricacies of coercive diplomacy is to delve into the realms of power projection, negotiation, and the subtle art of leveraging one's strengths to achieve strategic goals while avoiding open conflict.

1. Definition and Conceptual Framework: Coercive diplomacy can be defined as the deliberate use of threats, sanctions, or limited military actions to persuade a target state to modify its behavior, policies, or objectives. It operates within the gray area between peaceful negotiation and overt aggression, relying on the psychological impact of implied consequences to achieve diplomatic ends.

2. Historical Context and Evolution: The roots of coercive diplomacy can be traced through history, with nations employing a variety of methods to coerce adversaries or rivals into compliance. From the strategic demands of ancient empires to the Cold War era's nuclear brinkmanship, the evolution of coercive diplomacy reflects changes in global power dynamics, military technologies, and diplomatic strategies.

3. Instruments of Coercion: Coercive diplomacy employs a diverse array of instruments to exert pressure on a target nation.

These can include economic sanctions, diplomatic isolation, cyber operations, military posturing, intelligence maneuvers, and the strategic use of information warfare. The choice of instruments depends on the nature of the conflict, the goals of the coercing nation, and the perceived vulnerabilities of the target.

4. Economic Coercion: Economic tools are often central to coercive diplomacy. Economic sanctions, trade restrictions, and financial measures can cripple a nation's economy, prompting it to reconsider its policies or actions. The art lies in crafting measures that maximize impact while minimizing collateral damage and international blowback.

5. Military Posturing and Readiness: The visible demonstration of military capabilities and readiness is a classic component of coercive diplomacy. Through military exercises, strategic deployments, or the mobilization of forces, nations can signal their preparedness to respond decisively if diplomatic overtures are not heeded. The aim is to instill a sense of vulnerability and uncertainty in the target.

6. Diplomatic Isolation and Alliances: Diplomatic isolation involves rallying international support to isolate a target nation diplomatically. Coercive diplomacy often leverages alliances and coalitions to amplify the pressure on the target. By cultivating a united front, the coercing nation aims to present a formidable and united stance against the perceived transgressions of the target.

7. Psychological Warfare and Information Operations: The psychological dimension of coercive diplomacy is significant. Information warfare, propaganda, and psychological operations are employed to shape perceptions, influence public opinion, and create a narrative that reinforces the coercing nation's stance. The manipulation of information can sow doubt, dissent, or anxiety within the target nation.

8. Red Lines and Credible Threats: Coercive diplomacy

relies on the establishment of red lines—clear boundaries that, if crossed by the target, trigger a predetermined response. The effectiveness of coercive threats hinges on their credibility. A coercing nation must convincingly communicate its commitment to follow through on stated consequences, reinforcing the seriousness of its intent.

9. Exit Strategies and Face-Saving Measures: Successful coercive diplomacy often includes the provision of face-saving measures for the target nation. By offering a way for the target to de-escalate without losing dignity, the coercing nation enhances the likelihood of a diplomatic resolution while avoiding a scenario where the target feels compelled to resist pressure at all costs.

10. Regional and Global Power Dynamics: The success of coercive diplomacy is influenced by regional and global power dynamics. The alignment of other nations, the balance of power, and the strategic interests of key players contribute to the overall context within which coercive tactics unfold. A coercing nation must navigate these dynamics to build support for its objectives and mitigate potential opposition.

11. Case Studies in Coercive Diplomacy: Numerous historical and contemporary examples illustrate the application of coercive diplomacy. The Cuban Missile Crisis, where the U.S. and the Soviet Union engaged in a high-stakes game of nuclear brinkmanship, and the more recent use of economic sanctions against Iran to curb its nuclear ambitions are instances where coercive diplomacy played a central role in shaping outcomes.

12. Escalation Risks and Unintended Consequences: Coercive diplomacy carries inherent risks, including the potential for unintended escalation. The delicate balance between signaling resolve and avoiding a descent into open conflict requires careful calculation. Misjudgments, misunderstandings, or the failure to gauge the target nation's threshold can lead to unintended consequences.

13. Ethical Considerations and International Law: Coercive diplomacy raises ethical considerations and prompts scrutiny within the framework of international law. The use of coercive tactics must navigate the principles of proportionality, non-aggression, and respect for sovereignty. Violations of these principles can lead to accusations of aggression and impact the coercing nation's standing on the international stage.

14. Challenges of Multilateral Coercion: Coercive diplomacy becomes more complex in a multilateral context. Coordinating the actions of multiple nations, each with its own priorities and interests, requires adept diplomacy. Building consensus, managing divergent goals, and ensuring a united front are significant challenges in multilateral coercive efforts.

15. Economic Interdependence and Coercion: Economic interdependence adds a layer of complexity to coercive diplomacy. Coercing nations must consider the interconnectedness of global economies and the potential for mutual harm. Unilateral economic measures may be less effective if the coercing nation risks substantial economic fallout or if the target can find alternative partners.

16. Future Trends in Coercive Diplomacy: The future of coercive diplomacy is shaped by emerging technologies, evolving geopolitical landscapes, and shifting power dynamics. Cyber capabilities, space-based assets, and the integration of artificial intelligence in strategic planning are likely to play increasingly prominent roles. The adaptability of coercive tactics to these changing dynamics will influence their effectiveness in the years ahead.

17. Humanitarian Considerations and Coercive Measures: Coercive measures, particularly economic sanctions, often impact civilian populations. The ethical dimension of coercive diplomacy involves balancing the pursuit of diplomatic objectives with the humanitarian consequences of imposed measures. Addressing the potential suffering of innocent civilians is a critical aspect of ethical decision-making in coercive strategies.

18. Diplomatic Off-Ramps and Conflict Resolution: Successful coercive diplomacy should include diplomatic off-ramps—clear pathways for the target nation to de-escalate and engage in constructive dialogue. The ultimate goal is not only to coerce compliance but to create conditions for conflict resolution, fostering a stable and sustainable diplomatic outcome.

In conclusion, coercive diplomacy represents a subtle and intricate art within the realm of international relations. As nations navigate the complexities of the geopolitical stage, the strategic application of pressure without resorting to overt conflict becomes a hallmark of diplomatic finesse. The effectiveness of coercive diplomacy lies not only in the tactical deployment of instruments but in the ability to understand the nuances of power, psychology, and diplomacy to achieve desired outcomes while preserving global stability.

CHAPTER 13: BALANCING ACTS: THE DELICATE EQUILIBRIUM OF POWER

In the complex arena of international relations, the concept of "Balancing Acts" encapsulates the intricate dance of nations as they navigate the delicate equilibrium of power. This dynamic involves the strategic management of relationships, alliances, and resources to maintain stability, prevent dominance by any single power, and foster a multipolar world. Understanding the delicate equilibrium of power requires an exploration of historical precedents, geopolitical strategies, economic interdependencies, and the evolving nature of global dynamics in an interconnected world.

1. Historical Roots and Evolution: The roots of balancing acts can be traced through the annals of history. Ancient empires, medieval kingdoms, and early modern states engaged in balancing strategies to prevent hegemonic dominance by a single power. The evolution of this concept has adapted to the changing dynamics of warfare, diplomacy, and global interdependence.

2. Balance of Power Theory: The balance of power theory, a fundamental concept in international relations, posits that stability is achieved when power is distributed among multiple actors rather than concentrated in one. Nations strategically align or counterbalance against emerging threats, ensuring that no single entity can exert overwhelming influence over the international system.

3. Multipolarity, Bipolarity, and Unipolarity: The delicate equilibrium of power manifests in different forms depending on the distribution of power. Multipolarity, where multiple major powers coexist, fosters a balance through shifting alliances. Bipolarity, exemplified during the Cold War, involves a balance between two superpowers. Unipolarity, when a single power dominates, challenges the equilibrium and may prompt balancing acts to prevent unchecked influence.

4. Economic Interdependencies and Soft Power: Economic interdependencies play a crucial role in balancing acts. Nations engage in economic alliances, trade partnerships, and investment relationships to foster mutual dependence, creating incentives for peaceful cooperation. Soft power, including cultural influence, diplomatic finesse, and global appeal, becomes a tool for shaping international relations without resorting to overt coercion.

5. Alliances and Strategic Partnerships: Balancing acts involve the formation of alliances and strategic partnerships. Nations align with like-minded entities to pool resources, share security burdens, and counterbalance potential threats. The intricacies of these alliances require diplomatic skill to manage conflicting interests and maintain a collective sense of purpose.

6. Military Posturing and Deterrence: The delicate equilibrium of power is often reinforced through military posturing and deterrence. Nations invest in defense capabilities to signal resolve, deter potential aggressors, and maintain a balance of power. The strategic deployment of forces and the possession of advanced technologies contribute to the deterrence equation.

7. Regional Power Dynamics: Balancing acts are not confined to the global stage but extend to regional power dynamics. Nations in specific geographic regions engage in balancing strategies to prevent regional hegemony and maintain stability. The Arab states' balancing acts in the Middle East or the nations of Southeast Asia navigating the influence of major powers are illustrative examples.

8. Nuclear Deterrence and Arms Control: The advent of nuclear weapons introduces a unique dimension to balancing acts.

The concept of mutually assured destruction (MAD) underlines the equilibrium maintained through nuclear deterrence. International efforts at arms control seek to manage the delicate balance of power by preventing the proliferation of nuclear weapons.

9. Technological Advancements and Emerging Threats: The rapid pace of technological advancements introduces new elements into balancing acts. Cyber capabilities, space exploration, and artificial intelligence become arenas where nations seek to gain a strategic edge. The management of emerging threats and the prevention of technological imbalances contribute to the delicate equilibrium of power.

10. Global Governance and International Institutions: International institutions, such as the United Nations, act as platforms for diplomatic dialogue and conflict resolution. While these institutions aim to foster cooperation and prevent conflicts, they also play a role in the balancing acts of major powers, serving as arenas for strategic maneuvering and influence.

11. Economic Sanctions and Coercive Diplomacy: Balancing acts include the strategic use of economic sanctions and coercive diplomacy. Nations may impose sanctions to curb the influence of perceived adversaries, disrupt their economic stability, or coerce policy changes. The effectiveness of these measures hinges on the delicate calibration of pressure without provoking a destructive response.

12. Energy Security and Resource Competition: The quest for energy security and competition for vital resources contribute to balancing acts. Nations strategically engage in resource partnerships, invest in alternative energy, and seek to control critical resources to reduce vulnerabilities and ensure a stable supply chain.

13. Soft Balancing and Norm Entrepreneurship: Soft balancing involves the use of norm entrepreneurship and the shaping of international norms to counterbalance powerful actors. Nations may engage in norm-setting activities, diplomatic initiatives, and advocacy for global governance structures to constrain the behavior of dominant powers and maintain a delicate equilibrium.

14. Humanitarian Interventions and Ethical Considerations: Balancing acts intersect with humanitarian interventions, where the ethical considerations of power dynamics come to the forefront. The delicate equilibrium involves navigating the tension between non-interference and the responsibility to protect, with nations weighing ethical imperatives against national interests.

15. Cultural Diplomacy and Public Opinion: The soft power dimension of balancing acts extends to cultural diplomacy and the influence of public opinion. Nations leverage cultural exchanges, educational initiatives, and media outreach to shape perceptions, build goodwill, and foster an environment conducive to international cooperation.

16. Shifting Alliances and Geostrategic Realignment: The geopolitical landscape is dynamic, marked by shifting alliances and geostrategic realignment. Balancing acts require nations to adapt to changing circumstances, reassess alliances, and cultivate new partnerships based on emerging geopolitical realities.

17. Rise of Non-State Actors and Transnational Challenges: The rise of non-state actors, including multinational corporations, non-governmental organizations, and transnational networks, introduces new complexities to balancing acts. These entities wield influence beyond traditional diplomatic channels, challenging the equilibrium of power in unforeseen ways.

18. Challenges of Global Commons and Environmental Cooperation: Balancing acts extend to the management of global commons, including the oceans, outer space, and the environment. Nations must navigate cooperation and competition in these shared spaces, addressing challenges such as climate change, biodiversity loss, and the sustainable use of resources.

In conclusion, balancing acts epitomize the delicate equilibrium of power that nations strive to maintain in the intricate tapestry of international relations. This dynamic interplay involves strategic calculations, diplomatic finesse, and a constant reassessment of geopolitical realities. Navigating the delicate equilibrium requires adept leaders, skilled diplomats, and a nuanced understanding of the multifaceted factors that contribute to global stability. As nations continue to engage in this perpetual dance, the delicate equilibrium of power remains a cornerstone of the ever-evolving landscape of international relations.

CHAPTER 14: CRYPTIC ALLIANCES: NAVIGATING GEOPOLITICAL NETWORKS

In the intricate landscape of international relations, the concept of "Cryptic Alliances" unfolds as a complex tapestry of covert connections, hidden collaborations, and clandestine networks that operate beneath the surface of traditional diplomacy. These alliances, shrouded in secrecy, involve states and non-state actors engaging in strategic partnerships, intelligence-sharing, and coordinated actions to advance shared interests. Navigating the web of geopolitical networks requires an exploration of historical antecedents, the role of intelligence agencies, the impact on global dynamics, and the challenges posed to traditional concepts of diplomacy and international order.

1. Historical Precedents: Cryptic alliances have historical roots, with clandestine networks shaping the outcomes of conflicts and negotiations. The intrigues of espionage during the Cold War, covert collaborations during World War II, and secret agreements in the aftermath of major international events underscore the enduring nature of hidden alliances in the annals of geopolitics.

2. Intelligence Agencies and Covert Operations: Cryptic alliances often involve intelligence agencies playing a central role. These agencies engage in covert operations, information gathering, and clandestine collaborations with counterparts in other nations. The intelligence community becomes a key player in navigating geopolitical networks, influencing decisions, and shaping the strategic landscape.

3. Dual-Use Diplomacy and Secrecy: Dual-use diplomacy refers to the practice of states engaging in both overt and covert diplomatic activities. Cryptic alliances thrive on the duality of diplomatic engagement, where public statements and official channels coexist with covert collaborations conducted in secret. This dual-use approach allows states to pursue strategic objectives without revealing their full hand.

4. Non-State Actors and Covert Influence: Cryptic alliances extend beyond the realm of states to include non-state actors such as multinational corporations, non-governmental organizations, and powerful individuals. These entities leverage their influence to shape geopolitical outcomes through discreet collaborations, economic incentives, and behind-the-scenes maneuvering.

5. Proxy Warfare and Deniable Operations: Cryptic alliances often manifest in proxy warfare and deniable operations. States may support proxy groups or engage in actions that can be plausibly denied, creating a buffer of deniability while still pursuing strategic objectives. This allows for the projection of power without the overt attribution of actions to specific states.

6. Economic Espionage and Industrial Alliances: Economic espionage is a facet of cryptic alliances where states seek to gain a competitive edge through covert means. Industrial espionage, technology theft, and the covert transfer of economic intelligence contribute to the formation of alliances aimed at economic dominance and technological superiority.

7. Cyber Warfare and Information Operations: Cryptic alliances leverage the tools of cyber warfare and information operations to achieve strategic goals. States engage in covert cyber activities, including hacking, disinformation campaigns, and the manipulation of information flows. The interconnected nature of the digital realm provides fertile ground for clandestine collaborations.

8. Covert Alliances in Multilateral Institutions: Cryptic alliances extend into multilateral institutions, where states collaborate behind closed doors to influence decision-making processes. Covert lobbying, manipulation of international organizations, and the formation of secret blocs within institutions contribute to the complexity of navigating geopolitical networks.

9. Unconventional Alliances and Regional Power Dynamics: Unconventional alliances emerge in regional power dynamics, where states form cryptic partnerships to counterbalance perceived threats or advance shared regional interests. These alliances may transcend traditional geopolitical fault lines, creating shifting and unpredictable dynamics that challenge conventional notions of alliances.

10. Nuclear Proliferation and Covert Cooperation: Cryptic alliances play a role in nuclear proliferation, where states collaborate in secret to develop or acquire nuclear capabilities. Covert cooperation in the realm of nuclear technology and weapons development introduces a dangerous dimension to geopolitical networks, with the potential for destabilizing global security.

11. Non-Alignment and Strategic Ambiguity: Some states adopt a policy of non-alignment or strategic ambiguity, refraining from formal alliances while engaging in cryptic collaborations with various actors based on evolving circumstances. This approach allows for flexibility in navigating the geopolitical landscape without committing to overt alliances.

12. Regional Conflicts and Hidden Support: Cryptic alliances often manifest in regional conflicts, where states provide covert support to factions or governments without overtly intervening. The use of proxy actors, clandestine military assistance, and hidden logistical support contribute to the complexity of regional conflicts.

13. Countering Cryptic Alliances: Countering cryptic alliances presents significant challenges for states and the international community. Enhanced intelligence capabilities, robust cybersecurity measures, diplomatic initiatives to expose covert activities, and the strengthening of international norms against covert collaborations are essential components of countering cryptic alliances.

14. The Ethical Dilemma of Cryptic Alliances: Cryptic alliances raise ethical dilemmas related to transparency, accountability, and adherence to international norms. The covert nature of these collaborations can lead to abuses of power, human rights violations, and actions that undermine the principles of a just and equitable world order.

15. Geoeconomic Strategies and Cryptic Alliances: Geoeconomic considerations influence the formation of cryptic alliances. States engage in economic collaborations, currency manipulations, and trade agreements in ways that may not be immediately evident. Geoeconomic strategies become integral to the covert pursuit of geopolitical objectives.

16. The Role of Public Opinion: Public opinion plays a role in navigating cryptic alliances. The revelation of covert collaborations can have significant repercussions on the domestic front, affecting public trust in leadership and the legitimacy of state actions. Managing public perception becomes a crucial aspect of covert diplomacy.

17. Climate of Mistrust and Information Asymmetry: Cryptic alliances contribute to a climate of mistrust in international relations. Information asymmetry, where states possess hidden knowledge about covert activities, exacerbates tensions and complicates efforts to build genuine diplomatic relationships based on transparency and openness.

18. The Future of Cryptic Alliances: The future of cryptic alliances is shaped by technological advancements, evolving geopolitical landscapes, and the adaptability of states to changing circumstances. The integration of artificial intelligence, quantum technologies, and the continued convergence of the physical and digital realms will influence the nature and effectiveness of cryptic collaborations.

In conclusion, cryptic alliances form a shadowy undercurrent in the world of international relations, challenging traditional concepts of diplomacy and alliances. As states navigate the intricate web of geopolitical networks, the covert pursuit of strategic objectives introduces a layer of complexity that demands careful analysis, diplomatic acumen, and a commitment to ethical governance. The delicate dance of cryptic alliances continues to shape the global landscape, highlighting the need for vigilance, transparency, and international cooperation to navigate the hidden currents of international relations.

CHAPTER 15: ECONOMIC ESPIONAGE: THE SILENT BATTLE FOR RESOURCES

In the complex theater of global affairs, the term "Economic Espionage" emerges as a clandestine strategy that extends beyond traditional statecraft, marking the covert pursuit of economic advantages through illicit means. This silent battle for resources involves the theft, acquisition, or manipulation of proprietary information, trade secrets, and technological innovations to gain a competitive edge in the global marketplace. Understanding economic espionage requires an exploration of historical contexts, technological dimensions, geopolitical implications, counterintelligence efforts, and the evolving nature of this covert battleground.

1. Historical Context and Evolution: Economic espionage has deep historical roots, intertwining with the broader practice of espionage. Throughout history, states and entities sought economic advantages through covert means, with examples ranging from the theft of industrial secrets during the Industrial Revolution to the efforts of intelligence agencies during the Cold War to gain insights into economic policies and technologies.

2. The Nature of Economic Espionage: Economic espionage involves the clandestine collection of information related to the economic activities of a target, including trade secrets, intellectual property, financial strategies, and technological advancements. The perpetrators, often state-sponsored intelligence agencies or corporate entities, seek to gain a competitive edge, enhance economic capabilities, or undermine rivals in the global marketplace.

3. Motivations and Objectives: The motivations behind economic espionage are diverse and may include gaining access to advanced technologies, reducing research and development costs, acquiring trade secrets, manipulating commodity markets, securing a strategic advantage in negotiations, or undermining the economic stability of rival nations or corporations.

4. State-Sponsored Economic Espionage: State-sponsored economic espionage is a prominent aspect, where governments deploy their intelligence agencies to target foreign entities for economic gain. This form of espionage blurs the lines between traditional intelligence gathering and economic competition, as states use their resources to bolster domestic industries and weaken competitors.

5. Corporate Espionage and Industrial Sabotage: Corporate espionage involves businesses engaging in covert activities to gain an edge over competitors. This may include the theft of proprietary information, poaching of key personnel, or engaging in industrial sabotage to disrupt the operations of rivals. The line between state-sponsored and corporate economic espionage can often blur, with entities leveraging both state and corporate resources.

6. Technological Dimensions: The advent of the digital age has transformed economic espionage, with cyberspace becoming a primary battleground. Hackers, often state-sponsored or affiliated with corporate interests, target computer networks, databases, and communication systems to extract sensitive economic information. Cyber espionage is characterized by its stealth, sophistication, and potential for widespread impact.

7. Cyber Espionage and Advanced Persistent Threats (APTs): Cyber espionage often involves the use of advanced persistent threats (APTs), which are stealthy and continuous cyber-attacks designed to infiltrate systems, gather information, and remain undetected for extended periods. APTs are a hallmark of state-sponsored economic espionage campaigns seeking to maintain long-term access to sensitive data.

8. Intellectual Property Theft: Intellectual property theft is a common objective of economic espionage. This includes the unauthorized acquisition of patents, trademarks, copyrights, and other forms of intellectual property. Nations or corporations engaging in economic espionage may seek to replicate or reverse-engineer stolen intellectual property to gain a technological or economic advantage.

9. Supply Chain Exploitation: Economic espionage extends to supply chain exploitation, where adversaries infiltrate or compromise the production processes of targeted industries. By manipulating the supply chain, attackers can introduce vulnerabilities, compromise product integrity, or gain insights into manufacturing processes, disrupting the competitiveness of targeted entities.

10. Espionage in Emerging Technologies: Economic espionage intensifies in emerging technologies such as artificial intelligence, biotechnology, quantum computing, and renewable energy. The race for technological supremacy makes these fields particularly vulnerable to espionage, with nations seeking to gain an early advantage in the next frontier of innovation.

11. Economic Impact and Market Manipulation: The economic impact of espionage is far-reaching, affecting industries, markets, and national economies. Espionage can lead to market manipulation, unfair competition, and the erosion of trust in economic systems. Stolen information may be used to gain insider trading advantages or manipulate commodity prices.

12. Geopolitical Implications: Economic espionage carries significant geopolitical implications, as nations vie for economic dominance in the global arena. The covert acquisition of critical technologies, trade secrets, and economic strategies influences the balance of power, shapes international relations, and contributes to the emergence of strategic alliances and rivalries.

13. Counterintelligence and National Security: Counterintelligence efforts are crucial to thwart economic espionage and protect national security interests. Nations invest in detecting and preventing espionage activities, securing critical infrastructure, and enhancing cybersecurity measures to safeguard their economic assets from covert threats.

14. Legal Frameworks and International Cooperation: Establishing legal frameworks and fostering international cooperation are essential components of countering economic espionage. Nations collaborate to create legal mechanisms that facilitate the prosecution of economic spies, share threat intelligence, and develop norms that discourage illicit activities in cyberspace.

15. Challenges of Attribution and Deniability: One of the challenges in countering economic espionage is the attribution of attacks to specific actors. Perpetrators often seek to maintain deniability by using sophisticated techniques to conceal their identities. The difficulty in attributing attacks complicates the process of holding responsible parties accountable.

16. Economic Nationalism and Protectionism: Economic espionage can fuel economic nationalism and protectionist policies. Nations may respond to espionage incidents by adopting protectionist measures, restricting foreign investments, and intensifying scrutiny of international economic transactions to safeguard their industries and technologies.

17. Public-Private Partnerships: Public-private partnerships play a crucial role in combating economic espionage. Governments collaborate with private enterprises to share threat intelligence, enhance cybersecurity practices, and develop resilient strategies to safeguard economic assets from espionage threats.

18. Future Trends in Economic Espionage: The future

of economic espionage is shaped by evolving technologies, geopolitical shifts, and the adaptability of state and non-state actors. The integration of artificial intelligence, quantum computing, and advancements in cyber capabilities will likely define the next frontier of economic espionage.

In conclusion, economic espionage represents a silent battle for resources that transcends traditional notions of warfare and diplomacy. The covert pursuit of economic advantages through the theft of sensitive information challenges the fabric of international relations, requiring vigilant counterintelligence efforts, legal frameworks, and international cooperation to maintain the integrity of the global economic order. As nations grapple with the complexities of this silent battle, the evolving landscape of economic espionage continues to shape the destiny of industries, markets, and the geopolitical equilibrium.

CHAPTER 16: SILENT WARS: STRATEGIES BEYOND THE BATTLEFIELD

In the dynamic realm of international relations, the concept of "Silent Wars" unveils a multifaceted landscape where nations and actors engage in strategic maneuvers, subtle conflicts, and covert operations beyond the traditional battlefield. These silent wars encompass a spectrum of activities, including economic subversion, cyber warfare, intelligence operations, and psychological warfare, shaping the global order through means that extend beyond overt military confrontation. Understanding the intricacies of silent wars demands an exploration of historical contexts, contemporary manifestations, ethical considerations, and the evolving nature of conflict in the 21st century.

1. Historical Perspectives: Silent wars have historical antecedents deeply embedded in the annals of warfare and statecraft. Espionage, covert operations, and strategic subversion have been employed by states and non-state actors throughout history, from the ancient world to the Cold War era. The advent of modern technologies and the interconnectedness of the globalized world have, however, given rise to new dimensions in silent warfare.

2. The Silent Arsenal: Silent wars employ a diverse arsenal that extends beyond traditional military hardware. This arsenal includes cyber weapons, economic instruments, disinformation campaigns, propaganda machinery, covert intelligence networks, and unconventional tactics designed to exploit vulnerabilities in an adversary's systems, institutions, and societies.

3. Economic Subversion and Covert Strategies: Economic subversion forms a critical component of silent wars, where nations engage in covert strategies to undermine the economic stability of rivals. Economic espionage, trade manipulation, and the use of financial instruments as weapons contribute to a silent economic battleground that can cripple economies without firing a shot.

4. Cyber Warfare and Information Operations: The digital era has ushered in a new frontier of conflict with cyber warfare at its core. Silent wars leverage cyber capabilities to infiltrate critical infrastructure, disrupt communication networks, steal sensitive information, and launch coordinated attacks on a nation's digital assets. Information operations, including disinformation and propaganda, are key tools in shaping perceptions and influencing public opinion.

5. Hybrid Warfare and Blurred Boundaries: Silent wars often manifest as hybrid warfare, where a combination of conventional, unconventional, and non-military means are employed to achieve strategic objectives. The boundaries between war and peace become blurred, challenging traditional notions of conflict and necessitating a holistic approach to national security.

6. Intelligence Operations and Covert Networks: Intelligence operations form the backbone of silent wars, involving the collection, analysis, and exploitation of information to gain a strategic advantage. Covert networks, both state-sponsored and non-state, play a crucial role in gathering intelligence, conducting subversive activities, and influencing decision-makers on a global scale.

7. Psychological Warfare and Influence Campaigns: Psychological warfare is a subtle yet potent aspect of silent wars. Influence campaigns seek to manipulate perceptions, sow discord, and undermine the cohesion of adversaries. Propaganda, disinformation, and the use of social media platforms become powerful tools to shape the narrative and psychological landscape.

8. Proxy Wars and Surrogate Actors: Silent wars often employ proxy wars, where nations use surrogate actors to advance their interests without direct involvement. Supporting rebel groups, militias, or other non-state entities allows states to exert influence and project power while maintaining a degree of deniability.

9. Non-State Actors and Asymmetric Strategies: Non-state actors, including terrorist organizations and transnational criminal networks, are active participants in silent wars. Asymmetric strategies, where weaker actors exploit vulnerabilities in stronger adversaries, become prevalent, challenging traditional notions of military dominance.

10. Space and Electronic Warfare: Silent wars extend to space and electronic domains. Space-based assets are vulnerable to attacks, and electronic warfare capabilities can disrupt communication systems, radar networks, and other critical infrastructure. The militarization of space introduces a new dimension to silent warfare.

11. Ethical Considerations and Legitimacy: Silent wars raise ethical considerations regarding the legitimacy of unconventional tactics. Covert operations, cyber-attacks, and influence campaigns often operate in legal and ethical gray areas. Balancing the pursuit of national security interests with respect for international norms and human rights poses significant challenges.

12. Geopolitical Consequences and Global Dynamics: Silent wars have profound geopolitical consequences, shaping the dynamics of the global order. The use of covert strategies by major powers, rising actors, and non-state entities influences regional stability, alliance structures, and the balance of power, creating a complex and interconnected geopolitical landscape.

13. Countermeasures and Resilience: Nations must develop comprehensive countermeasures to navigate silent wars effectively. Building resilience against cyber threats, enhancing intelligence capabilities, fortifying critical infrastructure, and fostering societal resilience to disinformation are integral components of a nation's defense strategy.

14. International Cooperation and Norms: Addressing the challenges posed by silent wars requires international cooperation and the development of norms governing state behavior in the cyber domain, intelligence activities, and information operations. Building consensus on acceptable conduct in the digital age is crucial for preventing the escalation of silent conflicts into open hostilities.

15. Future Trends in Silent Wars: The future of silent wars is shaped by technological advancements, evolving geopolitical landscapes, and the adaptation of state and non-state actors to new realities. The integration of artificial intelligence, quantum technologies, and advances in biotechnology will likely redefine the contours of silent conflicts.

16. The Human Element and Cyber Resilience: Recognizing the human element in silent wars is essential. Cyber resilience involves not only technological safeguards but also educating individuals, organizations, and governments to recognize and counter the psychological and social engineering tactics employed in cyber warfare and influence campaigns.

17. Environmental Dimensions: Silent wars extend to environmental dimensions, where cyber-attacks can disrupt critical infrastructure, leading to environmental hazards. Additionally, the manipulation of environmental information and policies can be used as a tool in silent conflicts, affecting global efforts to address climate change and natural resource management.

18. Civilian Impact and Human Security: Silent wars have significant civilian impacts, affecting the daily lives of individuals. Disruptions to critical infrastructure, economic subversion, and the erosion of trust in information sources can compromise human security. Safeguarding the well-being of civilians becomes a paramount consideration in addressing silent wars.

In conclusion, silent wars represent a paradigm shift in the nature of conflict, challenging traditional notions of warfare and diplomacy. The silent battleground extends across multiple domains, requiring nations to adapt to the complexities of the 21st-century security landscape. As states navigate the intricate web of silent wars, the ability to blend technological prowess with ethical governance, international cooperation, and societal resilience becomes paramount in securing a stable and secure global future.

CHAPTER 17: THE SILENT OBSERVER: INTELLIGENCE AGENCIES AND GLOBAL AFFAIRS

In the complex tapestry of global affairs, intelligence agencies emerge as the silent observers, wielding significant influence behind the scenes. Operating in the shadows, these agencies play a pivotal role in shaping the geopolitical landscape, safeguarding national security, and influencing international relations. Understanding the intricate interplay between intelligence agencies and global affairs requires an exploration of historical contexts, the evolving nature of intelligence operations, ethical considerations, and the far-reaching implications of their actions on the world stage.

1. Historical Evolution: The roots of intelligence operations can be traced throughout history, from ancient civilizations employing spies to the intricate networks of espionage during the Renaissance. However, the formal establishment and professionalization of intelligence agencies gained prominence in the modern era, particularly during times of conflict such as World War I and World War II.

2. Intelligence as a Force Multiplier: Intelligence agencies serve as force multipliers for nations, providing decision-makers with critical information to enhance strategic advantage. The ability to collect, analyze, and disseminate actionable intelligence is a cornerstone of effective national security and foreign policy.

3. Roles and Functions: Intelligence agencies undertake a myriad of roles and functions, including but not limited to:

- **Collection of Information:** Gathering data through human intelligence (HUMINT), signals intelligence (SIGINT), imagery intelligence (IMINT), and open-source intelligence (OSINT).

- **Analysis:** Assessing collected information to provide accurate, timely, and relevant intelligence assessments.

- **Counterintelligence:** Protecting against espionage and ensuring the security of classified information.

- **Covert Operations:** Executing clandestine activities to achieve strategic objectives, ranging from covert support to allies to conducting operations against adversaries.

- **Cyber Operations:** Engaging in cyber activities to collect intelligence, disrupt adversaries, and defend national interests.

4. Intelligence and National Security: The primary mission of intelligence agencies is to safeguard national security. They provide early warnings of potential threats, assess the capabilities and intentions of adversaries, and contribute to the formulation of defense and security policies. The intelligence community is integral to a nation's ability to respond effectively to emerging challenges.

5. Coordinated Efforts and Interagency Collaboration: Intelligence agencies often operate as part of a broader intelligence community, involving multiple agencies working together to address complex security issues. Interagency collaboration is crucial for pooling resources, expertise, and intelligence assets to tackle multifaceted challenges that transcend borders.

6. The Cold War and Espionage: The Cold War era witnessed an intense rivalry between major powers, leading to extensive espionage activities. The intelligence agencies of the United States (CIA), the Soviet Union (KGB), and others engaged in a silent battle for information, with espionage becoming a defining feature of global affairs during this period.

7. Ethical Dilemmas and Oversight: Intelligence operations often raise ethical dilemmas, including concerns about privacy, human rights, and the potential abuse of power. Balancing the imperative of national security with the need for transparency and accountability requires robust oversight mechanisms, legislative frameworks, and adherence to ethical standards.

8. Intelligence Failures and Lessons Learned: The history of intelligence is marked by both successes and failures. Intelligence failures, such as the failure to predict the 9/11 attacks or the inaccurate assessment of weapons of mass destruction in Iraq, underscore the challenges and limitations of intelligence operations. These failures prompt a continuous process of evaluation and improvement within the intelligence community.

9. Technological Advancements: The digital age has transformed the landscape of intelligence, introducing new tools and challenges. Technological advancements, including artificial intelligence, machine learning, and advanced data analytics, enhance the capabilities of intelligence agencies in collecting, analyzing, and interpreting vast amounts of information.

10. Cyber Intelligence and Hybrid Threats: The rise of cyber intelligence has become a focal point in the modern era. Intelligence agencies engage in cyber operations to collect intelligence, disrupt adversaries, and defend national interests in the virtual realm. Hybrid threats, which combine conventional and cyber tactics, pose complex challenges that demand adaptive responses.

11. Global Reach and International Cooperation: Intelligence agencies operate globally, addressing transnational threats that require international cooperation. Collaborative efforts include information sharing, joint operations, and coordination to combat terrorism, cybercrime, and other global challenges that transcend national boundaries.

12. Role in Diplomacy: Intelligence agencies play an indirect yet influential role in diplomacy. The information they provide shapes diplomatic strategies, influences negotiation tactics, and contributes to the formulation of foreign policy. Shared intelligence can also serve as a basis for building alliances and partnerships.

13. Influence on Decision-Making: Intelligence assessments significantly influence the decision-making process of national leaders. Accurate and timely intelligence is critical for formulating effective responses to crises, making informed policy decisions, and navigating the complexities of international relations.

14. Countering Terrorism and Asymmetric Threats: In the post-9/11 era, countering terrorism has become a primary focus of intelligence agencies. The asymmetrical nature of contemporary threats requires agile and adaptive intelligence capabilities to anticipate, prevent, and respond to terrorist activities.

15. The Intelligence-Politics Nexus: The relationship between intelligence agencies and political leadership is intricate. While intelligence is meant to be apolitical, the interpretation and use of intelligence can be influenced by political considerations. Striking the right balance between independence and responsiveness to political leaders is a perennial challenge.

16. Future Trends in Intelligence: The future of intelligence is shaped by ongoing technological advancements, geopolitical shifts, and the evolving nature of threats. The integration of quantum computing, advancements in surveillance technologies, and the ethical implications of emerging capabilities will define the trajectory of intelligence operations.

17. Civil Liberties and Privacy Concerns: The collection of intelligence often involves the monitoring of communications and activities, raising concerns about civil liberties and privacy.

Striking a balance between protecting national security and respecting individual rights remains a delicate challenge for democratic societies.

18. Cultural Intelligence and Human-Centric Approaches: Recognizing the importance of cultural intelligence and understanding human behavior is increasingly crucial for intelligence agencies. Human-centric approaches, including empathy and cultural awareness, enhance the effectiveness of intelligence operations, particularly in navigating complex and diverse global landscapes.

In conclusion, intelligence agencies, as the silent observers of global affairs, wield a profound impact on the course of history. Operating discreetly in the shadows, these agencies navigate the complexities of the modern world, responding to emerging threats, shaping national security policies, and contributing to the delicate balance of power in international relations. The evolving landscape of intelligence reflects the perpetual challenge of adapting to new realities while upholding ethical standards and safeguarding the democratic principles that underpin the societies they serve.

CHAPTER 18: SILENT ECHOES: CULTURAL INFLUENCES ON DIPLOMACY

Diplomacy, often viewed as the formal conduct of international relations, is profoundly shaped by cultural nuances and subtleties that echo through the corridors of power. The term "Silent Echoes" encapsulates the unspoken cultural influences that permeate diplomatic interactions, from the intricacies of diplomatic protocol to the subtle dynamics of negotiation and communication. Understanding the profound impact of culture on diplomacy requires delving into historical contexts, exploring case studies, unraveling the layers of cross-cultural communication, and appreciating the role of cultural intelligence in navigating the complexities of international relations.

1. **Cultural Foundations of Diplomacy:** Cultural influences are deeply ingrained in the foundations of diplomacy. The practices of exchanging envoys, conducting rituals of statecraft, and engaging in diplomatic ceremonies have cultural origins that date back centuries. Diplomacy, as an institution, reflects the historical experiences, traditions, and values of nations.

2. **Diplomatic Protocol and Symbolism:** Diplomatic protocol, a set of formal rules and procedures, is steeped in cultural symbolism. From the manner of addressing dignitaries to the significance of gift-giving, every diplomatic gesture carries cultural weight. Understanding these subtleties is essential for diplomats to navigate the intricate dance of international relations.

3. **Historical Case Studies:** Examining historical case studies unveils the profound impact of cultural influences on

diplomatic outcomes. From the Treaty of Westphalia in 1648 to the Vienna Congress of 1815, cultural factors, including language, customs, and social norms, have played a decisive role in shaping diplomatic negotiations and agreements.

4. Cross-Cultural Communication Challenges: Cross-cultural communication is at the heart of diplomacy, and its challenges are manifold. Differences in language, non-verbal cues, and communication styles can lead to misunderstandings and misinterpretations. Culturally sensitive communication is crucial for building trust and fostering effective diplomatic dialogue.

5. Cultural Intelligence in Diplomacy: Cultural intelligence, the ability to understand and adapt to different cultural contexts, is a critical skill for diplomats. Diplomats with high cultural intelligence can navigate diverse cultural landscapes, build rapport with counterparts, and anticipate potential cultural sensitivities in negotiations.

6. Soft Power and Cultural Diplomacy: Soft power, the ability to influence through attraction and persuasion, often has cultural underpinnings. Cultural diplomacy, a subset of soft power, leverages cultural exchanges, arts, education, and language to foster mutual understanding and build positive relationships between nations.

7. Cultural Dimensions and Negotiation Styles: Cultural dimensions, as identified by scholars like Geert Hofstede, impact negotiation styles. Variations in power distance, individualism-collectivism, masculinity-femininity, and other dimensions influence how diplomats approach negotiations, make decisions, and navigate conflicts.

8. National Identity and Foreign Policy: Cultural influences shape national identity, and national identity, in turn, informs foreign policy. The perception of a nation's role in the world, its historical narratives, and its values all contribute to the formulation of diplomatic strategies and priorities.

9. Cultural Sensitivity in Conflict Resolution: Cultural sensitivity is particularly crucial in conflict resolution. Understanding the cultural roots of conflicts, acknowledging historical grievances, and respecting cultural identities are vital components of diplomatic efforts to mediate and resolve disputes.

10. Globalization and Cultural Hybridity: Globalization has brought about cultural hybridity, where nations and individuals are exposed to a multitude of cultural influences. Diplomacy in the 21st century must navigate the complexities of a globalized world, where cultural identities are fluid, interconnected, and dynamic.

11. Diaspora Diplomacy: Diaspora communities play a role in shaping diplomatic relations. Governments often leverage the influence of diaspora communities as cultural bridges, fostering connections and facilitating diplomatic initiatives between nations.

12. Cultural Challenges in Multilateral Diplomacy: Multilateral diplomacy involves navigating diverse cultural landscapes within international organizations. The United Nations, for example, brings together nations with varying cultural backgrounds, requiring diplomats to balance cultural differences while pursuing common goals.

13. Public Diplomacy and Cultural Narratives: Public diplomacy, aimed at influencing public opinion abroad, relies on cultural narratives. Cultural elements, such as films, literature, and popular culture, become tools for shaping perceptions and fostering goodwill between nations.

14. Cultural Influences on Alliances and Alliances: Alliances and coalitions are influenced by cultural affinities. Shared values, cultural similarities, and historical connections often underpin the formation of alliances, influencing diplomatic alignments and cooperation between nations.

15. Cultural Diplomacy in Crisis Management: In times of crisis, cultural diplomacy becomes a tool for building bridges and fostering international cooperation. The ability to convey empathy, understand cultural sensitivities, and communicate effectively is paramount in crisis management.

16. Technological Impact on Cultural Diplomacy: Technology has transformed the landscape of cultural diplomacy. Virtual exchanges, digital platforms, and social media play a role in facilitating cross-cultural interactions and shaping public perceptions on a global scale.

17. Cultural Influences on Global Governance: Cultural considerations impact global governance structures and institutions. The cultural perspectives of member states influence decision-making processes, priorities, and the effectiveness of international organizations in addressing global challenges.

18. Challenges and Opportunities for Cultural Diplomacy: The challenges of cultural diplomacy include avoiding cultural misunderstandings, addressing cultural biases, and adapting to the changing dynamics of cultural identities. However, these challenges also present opportunities for fostering mutual respect, building enduring partnerships, and advancing shared goals through cultural understanding.

In conclusion, the silent echoes of cultural influences on diplomacy resonate through the intricate tapestry of international relations. Diplomats, as stewards of their nation's interests, must navigate the subtle currents of cultural dynamics to build bridges, forge alliances, and foster mutual understanding in the complex arena of global affairs. As the world becomes increasingly interconnected, the role of cultural intelligence in diplomacy takes center stage, emphasizing the enduring importance of silent echoes in shaping the future of international relations.

CHAPTER 19: THE SUBTLE WEAPON: SOFT POWER IN GEOPOLITICS

In the intricate realm of international relations, the concept of "soft power" emerges as a nuanced and influential tool that transcends traditional military might and economic dominance. Coined by political scientist Joseph Nye, soft power represents the ability of a nation to shape the preferences of others through appeal and attraction rather than coercion or force. Understanding the dynamics of soft power in geopolitics necessitates a deep dive into its historical roots, the components that constitute it, its application in statecraft, the challenges it poses, and its evolving role in shaping the global order.

1. Historical Roots: Soft power, although a contemporary term, has historical antecedents. Throughout history, civilizations have wielded influence not only through military conquest but also through cultural, ideological, and diplomatic means. Ancient empires, such as the Roman Empire and the Chinese Han Dynasty, recognized the power of cultural exports and the spread of ideas in shaping their spheres of influence.

2. The Components of Soft Power: Soft power encompasses a multifaceted array of components, including:

- **Cultural Diplomacy:** Promoting a nation's cultural assets, including literature, arts, music, and language, as a means of fostering goodwill and understanding.

- **Public Diplomacy:** Engaging with foreign publics through various channels, such as media, educational exchange programs, and cultural initiatives, to build positive perceptions.

- **Ideological Attractiveness:** The appeal of a nation's political values, system, and societal model to others.

- **Economic Attraction:** The allure of economic opportunities, trade partnerships, and developmental assistance provided by a nation.

- **Institutional Influence:** The role of international institutions and alliances in projecting a nation's influence and values on the global stage.

3. The Soft Power Paradox: The paradox of soft power lies in its intangibility and the challenge of measuring its impact. Unlike military strength or economic output, soft power operates in the realm of perceptions, making it both powerful and elusive. The effectiveness of soft power often depends on the receptivity of the target audience and the authenticity of the narratives projected.

4. Cultural Hegemony and Global Influence: Soft power is closely linked to the concept of cultural hegemony, where the dominant culture of a nation shapes the cultural norms and preferences of others. Hollywood's influence, American popular music, and the global reach of English as a language are examples of cultural hegemony contributing to the soft power of certain nations.

5. The Role of Educational Exchanges: Educational exchange programs, such as the Fulbright Program, contribute significantly to soft power. By hosting foreign students and sending domestic students abroad, nations foster cross-cultural understanding, build networks, and create lasting connections that contribute to diplomatic goodwill.

6. Media and Information Dissemination: The media plays a pivotal role in projecting soft power. News outlets, entertainment industries, and social media platforms shape perceptions globally. Nations that control or significantly influence international media channels can leverage this influence to project their values and narratives.

7. Soft Power in Crisis Management: Soft power becomes particularly crucial in times of crisis. Nations that can project empathy, offer humanitarian aid, and demonstrate effective crisis management enhance their global standing. The response to natural disasters, pandemics, or international conflicts provides opportunities for nations to showcase their soft power.

8. Economic Statecraft and Development Assistance: Economic statecraft, involving the use of economic tools to achieve foreign policy objectives, is a significant aspect of soft power. Providing development assistance, investment, and trade opportunities can enhance a nation's attractiveness and influence in the international arena.

9. Soft Power and International Institutions: Participation in and influence over international institutions, such as the United Nations, the World Health Organization, and international financial organizations, contribute to a nation's soft power. Leadership in these institutions allows nations to shape global norms, standards, and regulations.

10. Soft Power Rivalries: Soft power is not only a tool for cooperation but also a source of rivalry among nations. Major powers engage in soft power competitions, vying for influence in regional and global affairs. This competition extends to cultural exports, media influence, and the promotion of competing ideologies.

11. Challenges to Soft Power: Soft power faces challenges, including:

- **Cultural Misunderstandings:** Cultural nuances can be easily misunderstood, leading to unintended consequences.

- **Authenticity Concerns:** Soft power is most effective when it is perceived as authentic. Attempts to manipulate or weaponize soft power can backfire.

- **Erosion of Trust:** Trust is essential for the success of soft power initiatives. Actions that erode trust, such as inconsistency in foreign policy, can undermine soft power efforts.

12. Soft Power and Democratic Values: Democracies often leverage their commitment to democratic values as a source of soft power. The appeal of democracy, human rights, and the rule of law contributes to the attractiveness of democratic nations on the global stage.

13. Technological Advancements and Soft Power: The digital age has reshaped the landscape of soft power. Social media platforms, digital communication tools, and online cultural content enable nations to reach global audiences directly, bypassing traditional gatekeepers.

14. Soft Power and National Security: Soft power and national security are intertwined. Nations that excel in projecting soft power can enhance their security by fostering positive relationships, gaining support in international conflicts, and mitigating the likelihood of military confrontations.

15. Cultural Diplomacy in Conflict Resolution: Cultural diplomacy plays a role in conflict resolution by fostering understanding, breaking down stereotypes, and creating platforms for dialogue. Cultural initiatives can contribute to building trust between conflicting parties and laying the groundwork for peaceful resolutions.

16. Soft Power and Regional Influence: Soft power is not limited to global influence; it also plays a significant role in regional dynamics. Nations can use soft power to build alliances, shape regional norms, and project influence in their immediate neighborhoods.

17. The Limits of Soft Power: Soft power has its limits. In situations where hard power considerations prevail or when dealing with adversaries resistant to influence, the effectiveness of soft power initiatives may be constrained.

18. Soft Power in Future Geopolitics: The future of geopolitics will likely see continued reliance on soft power as nations navigate a complex and interconnected world. The ability to adapt to technological changes, demographic shifts, and evolving global challenges will be key to maintaining and enhancing soft power influence.

In conclusion, soft power stands as a subtle yet potent weapon in the arsenal of geopolitics. As nations vie for influence, the ability to project attractive narratives, build genuine connections, and shape global perceptions becomes a strategic imperative. In an era where the lines between military, economic, and cultural power blur, soft power emerges as a dynamic force that shapes the course of international relations, contributing to the evolution of the global order in ways both seen and unseen.

CHAPTER 20: BEHIND CLOSED DOORS: SECRETIVE DIPLOMATIC NEGOTIATIONS

In the intricate dance of international relations, the art of diplomacy often extends beyond the public stage, finding expression in the confidential realm of secretive negotiations. The term "Behind Closed Doors" encapsulates the clandestine nature of diplomatic talks, where sensitive issues, delicate compromises, and strategic maneuvers unfold away from the scrutiny of the public eye. Understanding the dynamics of secretive diplomatic negotiations requires a comprehensive exploration of historical precedents, the motivations behind confidentiality, the tactics employed, ethical considerations, and the impact of such closed-door dealings on the global stage.

1. Historical Precedents: Secretive diplomatic negotiations have deep historical roots. From ancient empires to medieval kingdoms, leaders engaged in discreet talks to secure alliances, broker peace, or pursue strategic interests. Historical examples include the Treaty of Westphalia in 1648, where negotiations were conducted in secret to end the Thirty Years' War and reshape the European balance of power.

2. Motivations for Confidentiality: Several motivations drive diplomats and states to engage in secretive negotiations:

- **Sensitivity of Issues:** Issues involving national security, territorial disputes, or intelligence matters often demand confidentiality to prevent public panic or opposition.

- **Maintaining Flexibility:** Secrecy allows negotiators the flexibility to explore various options without being constrained by public expectations or scrutiny.

- **Building Trust:** Diplomats may need to establish trust with counterparts before publicizing agreements, ensuring that commitments are honored.

- **Avoiding Public Backlash:** Controversial or unpopular decisions may be easier to negotiate and implement if shielded from immediate public scrutiny.

3. Types of Secretive Diplomatic Negotiations:

- **Peace Treaties:** Historical peace treaties, such as those following major conflicts like World War I or the Korean War, often involved secretive negotiations to address complex issues.

- **Security Agreements:** Treaties or agreements related to defense, intelligence-sharing, or counterterrorism are frequently conducted behind closed doors.

- **Trade Negotiations:** Bilateral or multilateral trade agreements may begin with closed-door negotiations to address sensitive economic issues.

4. Tactics Employed in Secretive Negotiations:

- **Backchannel Diplomacy:** Envoys or intermediaries may be used for backchannel diplomacy, allowing discreet communication between parties.

- **Informal Meetings:** Informal settings and unpublicized meetings provide an environment for candid discussions without the pressures of formal negotiations.

- **Confidential Correspondence:** Written communication, often encrypted or delivered through secure channels, allows diplomats to exchange views and proposals discreetly.

5. The Role of Intelligence Agencies: Intelligence agencies often play a crucial role in secretive negotiations, providing decision-makers with critical information, conducting covert operations, and facilitating confidential communication channels between nations.

6. Ethical Considerations: The ethics of secretive diplomacy are complex. While confidentiality can be essential for effective negotiations, ethical concerns arise when decisions affect human rights, democratic principles, or when the public is intentionally misled.

7. Public vs. Private Interests: Balancing public and private interests is a perpetual challenge in secretive negotiations. Diplomats must navigate the tension between the need for transparency in democratic societies and the necessity of confidentiality in certain diplomatic endeavors.

8. Impact on Global Diplomacy: Secretive negotiations have a profound impact on global diplomacy. Successful closed-door talks can lead to breakthroughs in peace processes, the resolution of conflicts, and the forging of strategic alliances that reshape the geopolitical landscape.

9. Challenges in Maintaining Secrecy: The increasing interconnectedness of the world, advancements in technology, and the role of investigative journalism pose challenges to maintaining secrecy. Leaks, whistleblowers, or inadvertent disclosures can undermine the effectiveness of closed-door negotiations.

10. Case Studies:

- **Cuban Missile Crisis:** Backchannel negotiations between the United States and the Soviet Union, facilitated by intermediary countries, played a pivotal role in resolving the crisis.

- **Oslo Accords:** The secret negotiations between Israeli and Palestinian representatives in Oslo paved the way for historic agreements in the 1990s.

- **Iran Nuclear Deal:** The JCPOA negotiations involved confidential talks between Iran, the P5+1, and the European Union, highlighting the complex nature of nuclear diplomacy.

11. **The Role of Non-State Actors:** Non-state actors, including think tanks, advocacy groups, and influential individuals, may play a role in secretive negotiations by influencing decision-makers or facilitating discreet channels of communication.

12. **Humanitarian Considerations:** Secretive negotiations involving humanitarian issues, such as peace agreements in conflict zones, raise ethical dilemmas. Balancing the imperative for confidentiality with the need to address urgent humanitarian concerns requires delicate diplomacy.

13. **The Role of Diplomatic Immunity:** Diplomatic immunity plays a crucial role in protecting diplomats engaged in confidential negotiations. The Vienna Convention on Diplomatic Relations provides a legal framework to ensure the safety and security of diplomats.

14. **The Perception of Secrecy:** The perception of secrecy can influence how diplomatic negotiations are received by the public and the international community. A balance must be struck to ensure that secrecy enhances effectiveness without breeding mistrust.

15. **Lessons Learned from Past Negotiations:** Analyzing past secretive negotiations provides valuable lessons for diplomats, including the importance of trust-building, the need for contingency planning, and the recognition of the potential unintended consequences of closed-door decisions.

16. **Technological Advancements and Secrecy:** Advances in technology, including encrypted communication and secure digital platforms, offer new tools for maintaining confidentiality in diplomatic negotiations. However, these tools also pose challenges, as evidenced by cyber threats and hacking.

17. **Diplomacy in the Information Age:** In the information

age, where transparency is increasingly valued, diplomats must navigate the delicate balance between the demand for openness and the imperative of conducting effective closed-door negotiations.

18. Future Trends in Secretive Diplomacy: The future of secretive diplomacy will likely be shaped by evolving geopolitical challenges, technological advancements, and the ongoing tension between the necessity of confidentiality and the demand for transparency in a rapidly changing world.

In conclusion, the world of secretive diplomatic negotiations represents a fascinating and complex dimension of international relations. Behind closed doors, diplomats grapple with intricate challenges, weigh ethical considerations, and shape the course of history in ways that often remain unseen by the public. The delicate dance of secrecy in diplomacy underscores the nuanced nature of statecraft, where the ability to negotiate in confidence can be as critical as the outcome of the negotiations themselves, shaping the ever-evolving landscape of global affairs.

CHAPTER 21: THE SILENT CODE: DECIPHERING DIPLOMATIC LANGUAGE

In the intricate realm of international relations, the language of diplomacy is both an art and a science, often shrouded in nuance and subtlety. Referred to as "The Silent Code," diplomatic language serves as a sophisticated tool for communication, negotiation, and the projection of power. Understanding the intricacies of diplomatic language requires delving into its historical evolution, dissecting the components that define it, exploring the role of symbolism and ambiguity, analyzing the impact of cultural context, and considering the challenges and nuances that diplomats navigate as they engage in this subtle dance of words on the global stage.

1. Historical Evolution: The roots of diplomatic language can be traced back to ancient civilizations where emissaries and envoys were dispatched to convey messages between rulers. The modern form of diplomatic communication emerged during the Renaissance, with the establishment of permanent embassies and the codification of diplomatic practices.

2. Components of Diplomatic Language:

- **Formality and Protocol:** Diplomatic language is characterized by a high degree of formality and adherence to protocol. The choice of words, titles, and gestures is carefully calibrated to convey respect and avoid misunderstandings.

- **Precision:** Diplomats employ precise language to articulate their positions. Ambiguity is often intentional, but when clarity is required, diplomats rely on carefully chosen words to avoid misinterpretation.

- **Rhetoric:** The use of rhetoric allows diplomats to persuade, influence, and convey messages with impact. Well-crafted speeches and written statements are essential tools in diplomatic communication.

- **Coded Language:** Certain expressions or phrases may carry hidden meanings known to diplomats. These coded messages allow for discreet communication, especially in sensitive or covert negotiations.

3. Symbolism and Ambiguity:

- **Symbolic Gestures:** Symbolism is deeply embedded in diplomatic language. From the exchange of gifts to the arrangement of seating during negotiations, every action carries symbolic weight and conveys underlying messages.

- **Ambiguity:** Deliberate ambiguity is a hallmark of diplomatic language. Vague statements provide flexibility and allow for multiple interpretations, providing diplomats with strategic advantages in negotiations.

4. Cultural Context:

- **Cultural Sensitivity:** Diplomatic language is highly attuned to cultural nuances. Understanding the cultural context is crucial for diplomats to avoid misunderstandings, navigate differences, and build rapport with counterparts from diverse backgrounds.

- **Language as Identity:** The language chosen for communication reflects not only linguistic preferences but also national identity. Diplomats often use their native language as a statement of identity, emphasizing cultural pride.

5. Diplomatic Discourse:

- **Negotiation Language:** The language of negotiation involves a delicate balance between assertiveness and conciliation. Skilled negotiators employ techniques such as framing, bridging, and reframing to guide discussions toward favorable outcomes.

- **Multilateral Diplomacy:** In multilateral settings, such as international organizations, diplomats engage in discourse that must be inclusive and diplomatic, considering the diverse perspectives of participating nations.

6. Role of Silence:

- **Strategic Silence:** Silence can be a powerful tool in diplomatic communication. Strategic pauses, unspoken agreements, and the deliberate withholding of information contribute to the effectiveness of diplomatic language.

- **The Unspoken Message:** What is left unsaid can sometimes carry more weight than explicit statements. Diplomats may use silence to convey disapproval, signal readiness for compromise, or create suspense in negotiations.

7. Crisis Communication:

- **Crisis Diplomacy:** In times of crisis, diplomatic language becomes even more critical. Communicating resolve, reassurance, and the willingness to engage in dialogue is essential for preventing escalation and finding diplomatic solutions.

8. Public Diplomacy:

- **Addressing Global Audiences:** Diplomatic language extends beyond closed-door negotiations to address global audiences. Public diplomacy involves crafting messages that resonate with international public opinion, projecting a positive image of the nation, and countering negative narratives.

9. Challenges in Diplomatic Communication:

- **Translation Issues:** Language barriers and translation challenges can lead to misunderstandings. Diplomats must navigate linguistic differences to ensure that intended messages are accurately conveyed.

- **Balancing Act:** Diplomats face the challenge of balancing transparency with discretion. Striking the right balance between openness and confidentiality is crucial for maintaining trust in diplomatic relations.

10. Digital Diplomacy:

- **Social Media and Digital Platforms:** The advent of social media and digital communication has added new dimensions to diplomatic language. Diplomats now engage in digital diplomacy, using platforms such as Twitter to communicate directly with the public and shape narratives.

11. Soft Power and Persuasion:

- **Soft Power Diplomacy:** Diplomatic language is a key instrument of soft power. Persuasion, cultural influence, and the ability to shape narratives contribute to a nation's soft power, influencing how it is perceived on the global stage.

12. Crisis Narratives:

- **Shaping Narratives in Crises:** Diplomats play a critical role in shaping narratives during crises. Crafting messages that convey responsibility, empathy, and a commitment to resolution is essential for managing public perceptions.

13. Track II Diplomacy:

- **Informal Channels:** Track II diplomacy, involving unofficial and informal channels of communication, relies heavily on diplomatic language. These off-the-record discussions often play a role in building trust and exploring creative solutions to conflicts.

14. The Role of International Law:

- **Legal Language:** In the context of treaties, agreements, and international law, diplomatic language takes on a legal character. Precision in wording is crucial to avoid ambiguity and ensure the enforceability of agreements.

15. The Influence of Global Events:

- **Adapting to Global Changes:** Diplomatic language must adapt to global events and shifts in geopolitics. Responses to crises, emerging challenges, and evolving alliances require nimble and adaptive communication strategies.

16. The Ethics of Diplomatic Communication:

- **Truthfulness and Honesty:** While diplomacy often involves discretion, ethical considerations require diplomats to balance the need for confidentiality with principles of truthfulness and honesty.

17. Public vs. Private Diplomacy:

- **Strategic Messaging:** The divide between public and private diplomacy necessitates strategic messaging. Diplomats must consider how their public statements align with private negotiations, avoiding contradictions that may undermine credibility.

18. Future Trends in Diplomatic Language:

- **Digital Transformation:** The ongoing digital transformation is likely to shape the future of diplomatic language. Virtual diplomacy, online negotiations, and the use of artificial intelligence in language processing may become prominent features of diplomatic communication.

In conclusion, "The Silent Code" of diplomatic language is a complex and dynamic force that underpins the delicate dance of international relations. Whether in formal negotiations, crisis management, or public communication, diplomats navigate the intricate nuances of language to convey messages, build relationships, and shape the course of global affairs. As the world continues to evolve, so too will the language of diplomacy, adapting to new challenges, technologies, and geopolitical realities, while remaining rooted in the timeless principles of effective and strategic communication.

CHAPTER 22: IN THE SHADOWS OF CONFLICT: SILENT HUMANITARIAN DIPLOMACY

In the tumultuous landscapes of conflict, where the clashing of geopolitical interests often takes center stage, a quieter and equally critical dimension unfolds—Silent Humanitarian Diplomacy. This clandestine facet of international relations involves discrete, behind-the-scenes efforts to alleviate human suffering, negotiate access to conflict zones for aid agencies, and facilitate humanitarian interventions. Delving into the shadows of conflict, this form of diplomacy operates on the premise that human dignity should be preserved even in the direst circumstances. To understand the intricacies of Silent Humanitarian Diplomacy, one must explore its historical antecedents, the motivations that drive it, the challenges it faces, and its pivotal role in shaping the narrative of humanitarian assistance amid conflict.

1. Historical Roots: Silent Humanitarian Diplomacy has historical roots embedded in the efforts to provide relief during times of war. The International Committee of the Red Cross (ICRC), established in 1863, exemplifies early endeavors to protect and assist victims of armed conflicts. Over time, this humanitarian diplomacy evolved to encompass a broader array of actors, including non-governmental organizations (NGOs), UN agencies, and other entities dedicated to mitigating human suffering.

2. Motivations Driving Silent Humanitarian Diplomacy:

- **Preserving Human Dignity:** At its core, Silent Humanitarian Diplomacy is motivated by the imperative to preserve human dignity in the face of conflict. It seeks to ensure that vulnerable populations, often caught in the crossfire, receive essential assistance regardless of political or military considerations.

- **Mitigating Suffering:** The primary motivation is the alleviation of human suffering. Silent Humanitarian Diplomacy aims to negotiate access to conflict zones, secure the safety of aid workers, and facilitate the delivery of life-saving assistance to those in need.

- **Maintaining Neutrality:** Humanitarian actors operate under the principle of neutrality, emphasizing impartiality and independence. Silent Humanitarian Diplomacy seeks to navigate the complexities of conflict without becoming entangled in political or military agendas.

3. Components of Silent Humanitarian Diplomacy:

- **Negotiating Access:** Diplomats engaged in Silent Humanitarian Diplomacy work to negotiate access to conflict zones, often liaising with warring parties to secure safe passages for humanitarian aid.

- **Ensuring Safety of Aid Workers:** The safety and security of aid workers are paramount. Diplomats negotiate with conflicting parties to establish humanitarian corridors and guarantee the protection of those providing assistance.

- **Facilitating Dialogue:** Silent Humanitarian Diplomacy involves facilitating dialogue between humanitarian organizations, local authorities, and armed groups to overcome obstacles and ensure the unimpeded delivery of aid.

4. Challenges in Silent Humanitarian Diplomacy:

- **Access Restrictions:** Conflicting parties may impose access restrictions, hindering the delivery of humanitarian aid to those in need. Diplomats face the challenge of negotiating access in environments where political and military considerations often take precedence.

- **Security Risks:** Operating in conflict zones exposes aid workers to significant security risks. Silent Humanitarian Diplomacy must address these risks to ensure the safety of those delivering aid.

- **Political Sensitivities:** Humanitarian efforts can become entangled in political sensitivities. Diplomats engaged in Silent Humanitarian Diplomacy must navigate these complexities to maintain the impartiality and effectiveness of their interventions.

5. The Role of International Organizations:

- **United Nations:** The United Nations plays a pivotal role in Silent Humanitarian Diplomacy through agencies such as the United Nations Office for the Coordination of Humanitarian Affairs (OCHA) and the United Nations High Commissioner for Refugees (UNHCR). These entities engage in diplomatic efforts to coordinate humanitarian responses and ensure collaboration with host countries and conflicting parties.

- **International Committee of the Red Cross (ICRC):** As a key player in humanitarian diplomacy, the ICRC engages in discreet negotiations to access conflict zones, safeguard the rights of detainees, and ensure the protection of civilians.

6. Silent Diplomacy vs. Public Advocacy:

- **Maintaining Confidentiality:** Silent Humanitarian Diplomacy operates in the shadows to maintain confidentiality and discretion. This stands in contrast to public advocacy, where NGOs and humanitarian organizations often engage in public campaigns to raise awareness and garner support.

- **Strategic Use of Publicity:** In certain situations, strategically revealing information to the public may be part of Silent Humanitarian Diplomacy, aiming to draw attention to critical issues and garner international support.

7. Silent Diplomacy in Conflict Resolution:

- **Building Bridges for Peace:** Silent Humanitarian Diplomacy is not only about providing immediate relief but also about building bridges for peace. By engaging with conflicting parties and addressing the root causes of conflict, diplomats seek to create conditions for sustainable solutions.

8. Case Studies:

- **Syria:** Silent Humanitarian Diplomacy has been extensively employed in the Syrian conflict, where negotiators work to secure access to besieged areas, facilitate ceasefires for humanitarian corridors, and navigate complex political dynamics.

- **South Sudan:** In the context of South Sudan, diplomats engaged in Silent Humanitarian Diplomacy have grappled with challenges related to conflict-induced displacement, food insecurity, and ensuring the safety of aid workers.

9. Ethics in Silent Humanitarian Diplomacy:

- **Balancing Neutrality and Advocacy:** Maintaining the neutrality of humanitarian actors while addressing the ethical imperative to alleviate suffering poses ethical dilemmas. Silent Humanitarian Diplomacy must navigate this balance delicately.

- **Ensuring Accountability:** Diplomats engaged in Silent Humanitarian Diplomacy must ensure that their efforts do not inadvertently legitimize or condone human rights abuses. The accountability of conflicting parties is a key ethical consideration.

10. The Impact of Silent Humanitarian Diplomacy:

- **Saving Lives:** The primary impact of Silent Humanitarian Diplomacy is measured in lives saved. Negotiating access, securing safe passages, and facilitating aid delivery contribute directly to alleviating human suffering in conflict zones.

- **Building Trust:** Successful Silent Humanitarian Diplomacy builds trust between conflicting parties and humanitarian actors. This trust is essential for sustained access and effective collaboration.

11. Silent Diplomacy and the Media:

- **Navigating Media Sensitivities:** Silent Humanitarian Diplomacy must navigate media sensitivities, as the revelation of certain negotiations or interventions could jeopardize the safety of aid workers or compromise ongoing efforts.

12. Technological Advancements and Silent Diplomacy:

- **Secure Communication:** Technological advancements play a role in enhancing the security of communication in Silent Humanitarian Diplomacy. The use of encrypted messaging and secure digital platforms helps protect sensitive information.

13. The Role of Non-State Actors:

- **NGOs and Humanitarian Organizations:** Non-governmental organizations and humanitarian entities engage in Silent Humanitarian Diplomacy alongside governments. Their involvement often brings a grassroots perspective and a direct connection to affected communities.

14. Future Trends in Silent Humanitarian Diplomacy:

- **Digital Diplomacy:** The use of digital platforms for diplomatic communication may evolve in Silent Humanitarian Diplomacy, allowing for more efficient coordination and information sharing.

- **Inclusion of Local Actors:** Future trends may see increased collaboration with local actors and communities in Silent Humanitarian Diplomacy, recognizing their crucial role in conflict-affected areas.

15. Silent Diplomacy and International Law:

- **Humanitarian Principles in International Law:** Silent Humanitarian Diplomacy operates within the framework of international humanitarian law, which emphasizes principles such as humanity, neutrality, impartiality, and independence.

16. The Diplomacy-Humanitarian Nexus:

- **Synergy between Diplomacy and Humanitarianism:** Silent Humanitarian Diplomacy exemplifies the synergy between diplomacy and humanitarianism. It underscores the idea that addressing the human cost of conflict is not just a moral imperative but an integral part of conflict resolution.

17. Public Perception and Silent Humanitarian Diplomacy:

- **Shaping Public Narratives:** While Silent Humanitarian Diplomacy operates discreetly, shaping public narratives through strategic communication remains essential. Public perception can influence political will and support for diplomatic efforts to alleviate suffering.

18. Silent Humanitarian Diplomacy and Sustainable Development:

- **Linkages with Sustainable Development Goals (SDGs):** Silent Humanitarian Diplomacy aligns with various Sustainable Development Goals, particularly those related to ending poverty, ensuring good health and well-being, and promoting peace, justice, and strong institutions.

In conclusion, Silent Humanitarian Diplomacy stands as a vital and often unsung aspect of international relations, operating in the shadows of conflict to ensure that the plight of those affected by war is not forgotten. As conflicts persist and new challenges emerge, the role of Silent Humanitarian Diplomacy will continue to evolve, adapting to technological advancements, changes in global dynamics, and the imperative of upholding human dignity in the face of adversity. The silent diplomats working in this realm exemplify the commitment to a shared humanity that transcends borders and conflicts, embodying the hope for a more compassionate and just world.

CHAPTER 23: CYBERNETIC FRONTIERS: THE DIGITAL BATTLEFIELD

In the ever-evolving landscape of warfare, a new frontier has emerged—one that is intangible yet immensely potent: the Digital Battlefield. This cybernetic realm transcends traditional notions of conflict, featuring an intricate interplay of technologies, strategies, and vulnerabilities. To comprehend the complexities of the Digital Battlefield, it is imperative to explore its historical context, the elements that define it, the tactics employed, the challenges faced, and its profound implications on national security, geopolitics, and the very nature of warfare in the 21st century.

1. Historical Context: The genesis of the Digital Battlefield can be traced back to the early days of the internet and the advent of computer networks. However, its prominence surged with the increasing reliance on digital technologies in critical infrastructure, military systems, and everyday life. The Digital Battlefield has become a pivotal theater of operations, where conflicts are waged not only through traditional military means but also through cyberspace.

2. Elements of the Digital Battlefield:

- **Cyber Espionage:** Nation-states and non-state actors engage in cyber espionage to gather intelligence, steal sensitive information, and gain a strategic advantage. The Digital Battlefield serves as a playground for covert intelligence operations.

- **Cyber Attacks:** Offensive cyber operations involve targeted attacks on computer systems, networks, and infrastructure. These attacks can range from disrupting communication networks to sabotaging critical infrastructure, posing a significant threat to national security.

- **Information Warfare:** The manipulation of information has become a potent weapon on the Digital Battlefield. Disinformation campaigns, propaganda, and psychological operations are employed to shape narratives, influence public opinion, and sow discord.

- **Cyber Terrorism:** Non-state actors and extremist groups leverage the Digital Battlefield for acts of cyber terrorism. These may include attacks on financial systems, public utilities, or critical infrastructure to instill fear and create chaos.

- **Hybrid Warfare:** The Digital Battlefield often intersects with traditional forms of warfare in hybrid conflicts. Cyber operations are integrated with conventional military strategies to create a multidimensional approach to warfare.

3. Tactics Employed in the Digital Battlefield:

- **Malware and Ransomware:** Malicious software, including ransomware, is deployed to compromise systems, encrypt data, and extort victims. These tactics can cripple organizations, disrupt services, and impose significant economic costs.

- **Phishing and Social Engineering:** Cyber adversaries use phishing emails and social engineering techniques to deceive individuals into divulging sensitive information, such as login credentials or financial details.

- **Denial-of-Service (DoS) Attacks:** DoS attacks overwhelm targeted systems with a flood of traffic, rendering them unavailable. Distributed Denial-of-Service (DDoS) attacks amplify this impact by coordinating attacks from multiple sources.

- **Advanced Persistent Threats (APTs):** APTs involve sophisticated, long-term cyber campaigns orchestrated by well-resourced actors. These campaigns often target specific entities, such as government agencies or corporations, with the goal of prolonged, surreptitious access.

4. Challenges in the Digital Battlefield:

- **Attribution:** Determining the source of cyber-attacks is a persistent challenge. Cyber actors often employ tactics to obfuscate their origins, making it difficult to attribute attacks definitively.

- **International Norms and Laws:** The absence of clear international norms and legal frameworks for cyberspace complicates responses to cyber aggression. Defining what constitutes an act of war in the digital realm remains a complex and debated issue.

- **Dual-Use Technologies:** Technologies that have dual civilian and military applications pose challenges. Cyber capabilities developed for defensive purposes can easily be adapted for offensive use, blurring the lines between defense and offense.

- **Asymmetry and Non-State Actors:** The Digital Battlefield introduces asymmetry, where even non-state actors with limited resources can pose significant threats. This challenges traditional notions of military superiority and introduces a new level of complexity to national security.

5. The Role of Nation-States:

- **State-Sponsored Cyber Operations:** Nation-states engage in cyber operations to advance their strategic interests. State-sponsored attacks can range from intelligence gathering to disruptive and destructive actions, constituting a critical aspect of the Digital Battlefield.

- **Deterrence and Retaliation:** Establishing credible deterrence in cyberspace is a challenge. Unlike traditional warfare, the Digital Battlefield lacks clear rules of engagement, making it difficult to determine when and how to respond to cyber aggression.

6. The Human Element in the Digital Battlefield:

- **Cybersecurity Workforce:** The Digital Battlefield necessitates a skilled and agile cybersecurity workforce. Cyber defenders play a critical role in securing networks, identifying vulnerabilities, and responding to incidents.

- **Insider Threats:** Human actors, either wittingly or unwittingly, can pose significant threats in the Digital Battlefield. Insider threats may involve employees, contractors, or individuals with access to sensitive systems.

7. Critical Infrastructure Vulnerabilities:

- **Targeting Infrastructure:** Critical infrastructure, including power grids, transportation systems, and healthcare networks, is a prime target on the Digital Battlefield. Disrupting these systems can have cascading effects on society and national security.

8. Global Ramifications of the Digital Battlefield:

- **Geopolitical Implications:** The Digital Battlefield has profound geopolitical implications. Cyber capabilities have become integral to a nation's power projection, influencing diplomatic relations and strategic alliances.

- **Economic Impact:** Cyber-attacks can have severe economic consequences. The theft of intellectual property, disruption of business operations, and financial losses due to cyber incidents contribute to the economic impact of the Digital Battlefield.

9. Cybersecurity Resilience and Preparedness:

- **National Cybersecurity Strategies:** Nations develop comprehensive cybersecurity strategies to enhance resilience and preparedness in the face of cyber threats. These strategies encompass risk management, incident response, and international cooperation.

- **Public-Private Collaboration:** Cybersecurity in the Digital Battlefield requires collaboration between governments and private sector entities. Information sharing, joint exercises, and coordinated responses are essential components of this collaboration.

10. Ethical Considerations in the Digital Battlefield:

- **Non-Combatant Impact:** The Digital Battlefield raises ethical questions regarding the impact of cyber operations on non-combatants. Attacks on critical infrastructure can have far-reaching consequences for civilian populations.

- **Proportionality and Just War Theory:** Applying principles of proportionality and just war theory to cyber conflict becomes a complex task. Traditional frameworks for evaluating the morality of warfare must be adapted to the nuances of the Digital Battlefield.

11. Cyber Espionage and Intelligence Gathering:

- **Strategic Intelligence:** Cyber espionage plays a crucial role in gathering strategic intelligence. The Digital Battlefield allows for the surreptitious collection of information on military capabilities, geopolitical strategies, and economic activities.

12. Future Trends in the Digital Battlefield:

- **Artificial Intelligence (AI) and Machine Learning:** The integration of AI and machine learning into cyber operations will shape the future of the Digital Battlefield. Autonomous systems may play a role in both offensive and defensive capabilities.

- **Quantum Computing:** The advent of quantum computing poses both opportunities and challenges. While quantum-resistant encryption becomes imperative for cybersecurity, quantum technologies may also enhance offensive cyber capabilities.

- **Hybrid Threats:** The convergence of cyber threats with traditional threats creates hybrid challenges. Future conflicts may involve a seamless blend of conventional military actions, cyber operations, and information warfare.

13. International Cooperation and Diplomacy:

- **Norms of Responsible Behavior:** Diplomacy in the Digital Battlefield focuses on establishing norms of responsible behavior in cyberspace. International agreements, such as the Tallinn Manual, seek to provide guidance on the application of international law to cyber conflicts.

- **Cybersecurity Dialogues:** Bilateral and multilateral dialogues on cybersecurity contribute to diplomatic efforts to mitigate the risk of conflicts in the Digital Battlefield. These dialogues foster understanding, cooperation, and the development of shared norms.

14. Countering Disinformation:

- **Strategic Communication:** Countering disinformation is a key aspect of the Digital Battlefield. Strategic communication efforts aim to enhance public resilience, debunk false narratives, and mitigate the impact of information warfare.

15. Cybersecurity Awareness and Education:

- **Building Resilience:** Cybersecurity awareness and education programs are essential for building resilience at the individual, organizational, and national levels. Informed users and skilled cybersecurity professionals contribute to a more secure Digital Battlefield.

16. Regulatory and Legal Frameworks:

- **International Law in Cyberspace:** Developing robust regulatory and legal frameworks for cyberspace is an ongoing challenge. Nations grapple with defining the applicability of existing international law to cyber conflicts and exploring the need for new conventions.

17. Digital Warfare and Civil Liberties:

- **Balancing Security and Privacy:** The Digital Battlefield raises concerns about the balance between security imperatives and the protection of civil liberties. Governments must navigate the complexities of surveillance, data collection, and individual privacy rights.

18. Societal Implications of the Digital Battlefield:

- **Cybersecurity Culture:** The Digital Battlefield necessitates a cultural shift towards prioritizing cybersecurity. From individuals to organizations, cultivating a cybersecurity culture is crucial for collective defense against cyber threats.

In conclusion, the Digital Battlefield has become a defining feature of modern conflict, reshaping the nature of warfare and challenging traditional concepts of security. As societies, governments, and international actors grapple with the complexities of this cybernetic frontier, the imperative lies in developing adaptive strategies, fostering international cooperation, and embracing technological advancements responsibly. The Digital Battlefield is not confined to the realms of code and algorithms; it permeates the very fabric of global interactions, underscoring the need for a comprehensive and collaborative approach to navigate the challenges and opportunities it presents in the dynamic landscape of the 21st century.

CHAPTER 24: SILENT REVOLUTIONS: SOCIETAL CHANGES AND GLOBAL IMPACT

The phrase "Silent Revolutions" encapsulates a profound and often overlooked aspect of human history—incremental and transformative shifts in societies that, while lacking the dramatic flair of revolutions in the traditional sense, exert a significant and enduring impact on global dynamics. To comprehend the depth and breadth of these silent revolutions, it is essential to explore their historical origins, the driving forces behind them, the manifold manifestations across different societies, and the far-reaching implications they bear on culture, economics, politics, and the overall fabric of the interconnected world.

1. Historical Origins: Silent revolutions find their roots in the organic evolution of societies over time. Unlike the explicit and tumultuous nature of traditional revolutions, these shifts are characterized by gradual changes in attitudes, norms, and structures. Examples include the Industrial Revolution's transformative impact on economies and the Enlightenment's influence on thought and governance.

2. Forces Driving Silent Revolutions:

- **Technological Advancements:** The continuous march of technology often catalyzes silent revolutions. From the advent of the printing press to the rise of the internet, technological shifts reshape communication, commerce, and the dissemination of ideas.

- **Cultural Movements:** Movements advocating for civil rights, gender equality, and environmental sustainability exemplify silent revolutions in the cultural sphere. These movements challenge existing norms and foster more inclusive societies.

- **Economic Paradigm Shifts:** The transition from agrarian to industrial economies and the subsequent move towards a knowledge-based economy constitute silent revolutions with far-reaching economic implications.

- **Demographic Changes:** Shifting demographics, including urbanization and changing population structures, contribute to silent revolutions by altering social dynamics, consumption patterns, and political landscapes.

3. Manifestations Across Societies:

- **Social Equality Movements:** Silent revolutions often manifest in movements advocating for social equality. From the civil rights movement in the United States to the fight against apartheid in South Africa, these movements reshape societal norms and challenge systemic inequalities.

- **Digital Revolution:** The advent of the digital age is a contemporary silent revolution that transcends borders. It has transformed communication, commerce, and social interactions, fundamentally altering the way individuals and societies operate.

- **Environmental Consciousness:** The global shift towards environmental consciousness, marked by movements like climate activism and sustainable living practices, represents a silent revolution addressing the urgent need for planetary stewardship.

4. Impact on Culture:

- **Cultural Pluralism:** Silent revolutions contribute to the emergence of cultural pluralism, fostering greater acceptance of diversity in language, customs, and lifestyles.

- **Cultural Hybridity:** Increasing interconnectedness results in the blending of cultural elements, creating hybrid identities and fostering a globalized cultural landscape.

- **Individual Empowerment:** Silent revolutions empower individuals to express their identities authentically, challenging traditional norms and contributing to a more inclusive cultural sphere.

5. Economic Implications:

- **Knowledge Economy:** The shift towards a knowledge-based economy, marked by the rise of technology and information industries, represents a silent revolution with profound economic implications.

- **Globalization:** Economic globalization, facilitated by advancements in transportation and communication, is a silent revolution that intertwines economies, making them more interdependent.

6. Political Transformations:

- **Advancements in Governance:** Silent revolutions in political systems involve advancements in governance, including the spread of democratic ideals, the recognition of human rights, and the establishment of international institutions fostering cooperation.

- **Decentralization:** Movements towards decentralization and devolution of power represent a subtle but impactful transformation in political structures.

7. Social Movements:

- **Women's Rights:** The gradual but transformative expansion of women's rights, from securing suffrage to advocating for gender equality, represents a silent revolution with profound social implications.

- **Civil Rights:** Silent revolutions in civil rights have challenged systemic discrimination and promoted inclusivity and equality, reshaping the social fabric of nations.

8. Technological Innovations:

- **Digital Connectivity:** The digital revolution, marked by the rise of the internet and connected technologies, is a silent revolution with unparalleled impact on communication, information dissemination, and social interactions.

- **Biotechnological Advancements:** Innovations in biotechnology, from genetic engineering to medical breakthroughs, constitute a silent revolution in healthcare and the understanding of life itself.

9. Education and Knowledge Access:

- **Widespread Education:** Silent revolutions in education involve the democratization of knowledge, making education more accessible globally and empowering individuals irrespective of socio-economic backgrounds.

- **Online Learning:** The rise of online learning platforms represents a contemporary silent revolution in education, offering flexible and inclusive learning opportunities.

10. Impact on Power Structures:

- **Shifts in Global Power:** Silent revolutions contribute to shifts in global power dynamics, with emerging economies gaining influence and challenging established hierarchies.

- **Empowerment of Marginalized Groups:** Movements advocating for the rights of marginalized groups represent a silent revolution by challenging historical power imbalances and promoting inclusivity.

11. Environmental Consciousness:

- **Sustainable Practices:** The growing emphasis on environmental sustainability represents a silent revolution that reshapes consumer behavior, corporate practices, and policy agendas, reflecting a broader shift towards ecological awareness.

12. Challenges in Navigating Silent Revolutions:

- **Resistance to Change:** Silent revolutions face resistance from entrenched interests and individuals resistant to cultural, social, or economic transformations.

- **Pace of Change:** The pace of silent revolutions, sometimes gradual and incremental, may pose challenges in addressing urgent global issues.

13. Global Connectivity and Interdependence:

- **Interconnected World:** Silent revolutions contribute to an interconnected global landscape, where events and developments in one part of the world have far-reaching consequences across borders.

- **Global Challenges:** Issues such as climate change, pandemics, and economic crises require collaborative responses, highlighting the interdependence forged by silent revolutions.

14. Future Trajectories of Silent Revolutions:

- **Artificial Intelligence (AI) and Automation:** The integration of AI and automation into various facets of society represents a potential silent revolution with implications for employment, governance, and the very fabric of daily life.

- **Renewable Energy Transition:** The ongoing transition

to renewable energy sources signals a silent revolution in the energy sector, with implications for environmental sustainability and global geopolitics.

15. Ethical Considerations:

- **Ethical Dimensions of Change:** Silent revolutions necessitate ethical considerations, particularly regarding the impact of transformations on individuals, communities, and the planet.

- **Equitable Development:** Ensuring that the benefits of silent revolutions are distributed equitably raises ethical questions about social justice and inclusivity.

16. Cultural Preservation Amid Change:

- **Preserving Cultural Heritage:** As societies undergo silent revolutions, there is a need to balance progress with the preservation of cultural heritage and traditional practices.

17. Education and Awareness:

- **Promoting Understanding:** Education and awareness play a crucial role in navigating silent revolutions, fostering a deeper understanding of societal changes and their implications.

18. The Role of Leadership:

- **Guiding Transformations:** Leadership, both at the national and global levels, plays a vital role in guiding societies through silent revolutions, ensuring that the changes are managed effectively and responsibly.

In conclusion, silent revolutions, despite their subtle nature, form the undercurrents that shape the course of human history. As societies navigate the complexities of cultural, technological, and societal transformations, the understanding and proactive management of these silent revolutions become imperative for creating a more equitable, sustainable, and interconnected world. The silent revolutions of today pave the way for the world of tomorrow, highlighting the importance of embracing change while fostering a collective responsibility for the well-being of humanity and the planet we inhabit.

CHAPTER 25: ENVIRONMENTAL DIPLOMACY: SILENT AGREEMENTS FOR A SUSTAINABLE FUTURE

Environmental Diplomacy represents a critical intersection where international relations, ecological concerns, and sustainable development converge. In the pursuit of a sustainable future, nations engage in diplomatic efforts to address shared environmental challenges, negotiate agreements, and collaborate on policies that transcend borders. Often conducted behind closed doors, these negotiations and agreements form a category of diplomacy often referred to as "silent agreements," where the focus is on fostering environmental stewardship without the fanfare of traditional diplomatic achievements. To comprehensively understand Environmental Diplomacy and its role in shaping a sustainable future, one must delve into its historical context, the key actors involved, the challenges faced, the mechanisms employed, and the transformative impact on global environmental governance.

1. Historical Context:

- **Emergence of Environmental Concerns:** The roots of Environmental Diplomacy can be traced to the mid-20th century when the world began to grapple with the consequences of industrialization, pollution, and resource depletion. Early international agreements, such as the 1972 Stockholm Conference, marked the recognition of the global nature of environmental challenges.

2. Key Actors in Environmental Diplomacy:

- **United Nations:** The United Nations (UN) plays

a central role in Environmental Diplomacy through various bodies, including the United Nations Environment Programme (UNEP) and the Intergovernmental Panel on Climate Change (IPCC). These entities facilitate global cooperation, research, and the formulation of international environmental policies.

- **Non-Governmental Organizations (NGOs):** Environmental NGOs, such as Greenpeace and the World Wildlife Fund (WWF), contribute to Environmental Diplomacy by advocating for sustainable practices, conducting research, and often participating as observers in international negotiations.

- **National Governments:** Governments are pivotal actors in Environmental Diplomacy, representing their countries in negotiations, formulating policies, and committing to international agreements to address environmental challenges.

3. Silent Agreements and Informal Diplomacy:

- **Behind Closed Doors:** Silent agreements in Environmental Diplomacy are often negotiated behind closed doors, away from the public spotlight. This allows negotiators to engage in candid discussions and make compromises that might be challenging in a more public forum.

- **Informal Channels:** Informal diplomatic channels, such as private meetings and backchannel negotiations, are commonly employed to build consensus and address contentious issues discreetly.

4. Mechanisms of Environmental Diplomacy:

- **Multilateral Agreements:** Treaties and agreements negotiated in multilateral forums, such as the Paris Agreement and the Convention on Biological Diversity, are key mechanisms in Environmental Diplomacy. These agreements set out goals, targets, and frameworks for international cooperation.

- **Bilateral Agreements:** Nations engage in bilateral agreements to address specific environmental issues that may be unique to their geographic or geopolitical context. These agreements allow for tailored solutions to shared challenges.

5. Key Environmental Challenges Addressed:

- **Climate Change:** Perhaps the most pressing challenge, climate change negotiations form a substantial part of Environmental Diplomacy. The Paris Agreement, emerging from COP21, exemplifies a multilateral effort to combat climate change through global cooperation.

- **Biodiversity Loss:** Diplomatic efforts also focus on addressing biodiversity loss, with conventions like the Convention on Biological Diversity aiming to conserve biodiversity, sustainably use its components, and ensure the fair sharing of benefits.

6. Challenges in Environmental Diplomacy:

- **Divergent National Interests:** Balancing national interests with global environmental imperatives poses a significant challenge. Nations may prioritize economic development over stringent environmental regulations, leading to tensions in negotiations.

- **Scientific Uncertainty:** Disagreements arising from scientific uncertainties regarding the causes and impacts of environmental issues can complicate diplomatic efforts. Bridging these gaps requires nuanced negotiation and international collaboration.

- **Enforcement and Compliance:** Ensuring enforcement and compliance with international environmental agreements remains a persistent challenge. The absence of effective mechanisms to hold nations accountable can undermine the success of diplomatic efforts.

7. Success Stories in Environmental Diplomacy:

- **Montreal Protocol:** The Montreal Protocol, addressing the depletion of the ozone layer, stands as a success story in Environmental Diplomacy. The agreement led to a phased reduction of ozone-depleting substances, showcasing the potential for global cooperation in addressing environmental challenges.

- **Antarctic Treaty:** The Antarctic Treaty, signed in 1959, represents a successful environmental diplomatic effort. It designates Antarctica as a scientific preserve, prohibits military activity, and sets a precedent for collaborative environmental governance.

8. Environmental Justice and Equity:

- **Global South and North Dynamics:** Environmental Diplomacy often involves navigating the dynamics between developed and developing nations. The Global South may argue for historical responsibility and demand equity in shouldering the burden of environmental protection.

- **Indigenous Rights:** Indigenous communities, often disproportionately affected by environmental degradation, seek recognition in diplomatic efforts.

Integrating traditional knowledge and respecting indigenous rights emerge as crucial aspects of equitable Environmental Diplomacy.

9. Shifting Paradigms:

- **From Confrontation to Collaboration:** Environmental Diplomacy has evolved from confrontational approaches to collaborative strategies. Rather than pitting nations against each other, there is a growing recognition that global challenges require collective action and shared responsibility.

10. The Role of Technology:

- **Technological Innovation:** Technology plays a role in Environmental Diplomacy by offering innovative solutions to environmental challenges. This includes clean energy technologies, monitoring systems, and data analytics that inform evidence-based policy decisions.

11. Economic Considerations:

- **Green Diplomacy:** The intersection of economic and environmental interests is encapsulated in the concept of Green Diplomacy. Nations increasingly recognize that sustainable economic practices align with environmental goals, fostering a green economy.

12. Public Engagement and Advocacy:

- **Civil Society Activism:** Public engagement and civil society activism play a crucial role in shaping Environmental Diplomacy. Grassroots movements and public pressure can influence government policies and international negotiations.

- **Media Influence:** The media serves as a critical conduit between environmental issues and the public, influencing public opinion and, in turn, impacting the diplomatic decisions of governments.

13. The Future of Environmental Diplomacy:

- **Integration with Global Agendas:** Environmental Diplomacy is expected to become more integrated with broader global agendas, such as the Sustainable Development Goals (SDGs). The interconnected nature of environmental issues necessitates a holistic approach to sustainable development.

- **Innovative Financing:** Exploring innovative financing mechanisms, such as green bonds and climate funds, will be integral to addressing the financial aspects of environmental challenges.

14. Ethical Considerations:

- **Intergenerational Equity:** Environmental Diplomacy involves ethical considerations, particularly regarding intergenerational equity. Decisions made today impact future generations, necessitating a long-term perspective in diplomatic efforts.

15. Education and Capacity Building:

- **Building Diplomatic Capacity:** Diplomatic capacity in environmental matters is crucial. This includes training diplomats in environmental science, policy analysis, and negotiation skills to navigate complex and evolving environmental issues.

16. Regional Environmental Diplomacy:

- **Regional Cooperation:** Regional initiatives and agreements play a vital role in Environmental Diplomacy. They allow neighboring countries to address shared environmental challenges collaboratively, recognizing the interconnectedness of ecosystems.

17. Global Partnerships:

- **Public-Private Partnerships:** Engaging the private sector through public-private partnerships is increasingly recognized as essential in addressing environmental challenges. Businesses can contribute resources, innovation, and expertise to complement governmental efforts.

18. Silent Agreements as Catalysts for Change:

- **Incremental Progress:** Silent agreements in Environmental Diplomacy, while lacking the immediate visibility of more sensational diplomatic achievements, contribute to incremental progress. They represent the diplomatic subtleties required to navigate the complex terrain of global environmental governance.

In conclusion, Environmental Diplomacy stands as a silent force shaping the trajectory of humanity's relationship with the planet. As nations negotiate behind closed doors, silent agreements emerge as catalysts for a sustainable future, transcending geopolitical boundaries in the pursuit of a shared environmental legacy. The challenges are formidable, but the diplomatic endeavors, both seen and unseen, hold the potential to usher in a future where the delicate balance between human development and ecological preservation is maintained for generations to come.

CHAPTER 26: SILENT CATALYSTS: INDIVIDUALS SHAPING GLOBAL POLICY

In the vast tapestry of global affairs, certain individuals emerge as silent catalysts, wielding influence and shaping policies that resonate far beyond their immediate spheres. These figures, often operating discreetly behind the scenes, contribute to the development and transformation of global policies. Their impact transcends the public eye, as they navigate diplomatic channels, advocate for change, and craft strategies that resonate across international borders. To comprehend the intricate dynamics of these silent catalysts, one must delve into their historical precedents, the diversity of their roles, the strategies they employ, the challenges they face, and the lasting imprint they leave on the course of global governance.

1. Historical Precedents of Silent Catalysts:

- **Diplomatic Visionaries:** Throughout history, figures such as diplomats, strategists, and negotiators have played pivotal roles in shaping global policies. From Metternich in the 19th century to Kissinger in the 20th, these individuals navigated complex geopolitical landscapes, leaving enduring imprints on the international order.

- **Unseen Architects of Treaties:** Architects of seminal treaties, such as the drafters of the Treaty of Westphalia in 1648 or the framers of the United Nations Charter in 1945, functioned as silent catalysts whose work laid the foundations for modern international relations.

2. Diversity of Roles in Silent Catalysts:

- **Behind-the-Scenes Negotiators:** Silent catalysts often operate as behind-the-scenes negotiators, brokering agreements and compromises away from public scrutiny. Their diplomatic finesse enables them to bridge divides and find common ground.

- **Policy Architects:** Some individuals act as architects of policies that shape the global landscape. Whether in economic, environmental, or security domains, these architects craft frameworks that influence nations and international institutions.

- **Thought Leaders:** Silent catalysts include thought leaders who shape global policy by influencing public opinion and steering discourse. Their ideas permeate academic, political, and institutional circles, laying the groundwork for paradigm shifts in policy.

3. Strategies Employed by Silent Catalysts:

- **Network Diplomacy:** Establishing and nurturing networks of influence is a common strategy. Silent catalysts often leverage personal relationships, whether within diplomatic circles, business communities, or academia, to facilitate policy changes.

- **Strategic Communication:** Effective communication, sometimes through the media but often in more discreet forums, is a crucial strategy. Crafting narratives and framing issues enable silent catalysts to shape perceptions and garner support for their policy objectives.

- **Policy Entrepreneurship:** Silent catalysts engage in policy entrepreneurship by identifying gaps or inefficiencies in existing policies and proposing innovative solutions. This proactive approach allows them to drive change from within established systems.

- **Institutional Infiltration:** Some individuals strategically infiltrate international institutions, governmental bodies, or influential think tanks, enabling them to exert influence over policy decisions from within these structures.

4. Challenges Faced by Silent Catalysts:

- **Lack of Recognition:** Silent catalysts often work discreetly, leading to a lack of public recognition for their contributions. While their impact may be profound, it can go unnoticed outside diplomatic and policymaking circles.

- **Balancing Act:** Navigating the delicate balance between personal convictions and institutional frameworks poses a challenge. Silent catalysts must reconcile their ideals with the pragmatic considerations of international relations.

- **Resistance to Change:** Resistance from established interests, bureaucratic inertia, and geopolitical rivalries can impede the efforts of silent catalysts. Effecting change requires navigating complex political landscapes and overcoming entrenched opposition.

5. Enduring Impact on Global Governance:

- **Normative Shifts:** Silent catalysts contribute to normative shifts in global governance. Their efforts may lead to the establishment of new norms, principles, and standards that guide international behavior.

- **Institutional Innovations:** Some individuals play a role in crafting institutional innovations that reshape the architecture of global governance. This can include the creation of new international organizations or the reform of existing ones.

6. Case Studies of Silent Catalysts:

- **Dag Hammarskjöld:** The second Secretary-General of the United Nations, Dag Hammarskjöld, is regarded as a silent catalyst. His role in mediating the Suez Crisis and his commitment to UN neutrality left an indelible mark on the institution's role in conflict resolution.

- **Hedy Lamarr:** The Hollywood actress Hedy Lamarr made substantial contributions to technology and communication during World War II, co-inventing a frequency-hopping system that laid the groundwork for modern wireless communication technologies.

7. Cultural and Social Influences:

- **Cultural Catalysts:** Figures from cultural spheres, including artists, writers, and intellectuals, can be silent catalysts by shaping cultural narratives that, in turn, influence public opinion and policy directions.

- **Social Reformers:** Individuals championing social causes, such as gender equality or human rights, can act as silent catalysts by inspiring policy changes and influencing public attitudes.

8. Ethical Considerations:

- **Ethics in Diplomacy:** Silent catalysts grapple with ethical considerations, as their actions may involve navigating moral dilemmas in pursuit of strategic goals. The ethical dimensions of their decisions impact the legitimacy of their influence.

9. Technology and Information Age Influences:

- **Digital Influencers:** In the Information Age, digital influencers and activists can function as silent catalysts by leveraging online platforms to shape narratives, mobilize public opinion, and influence policymakers.

- **Tech Innovators:** Technological innovators who shape the digital landscape can be silent catalysts, influencing global policies on issues ranging from cybersecurity to data privacy.

10. Future Trajectories of Silent Catalysts:

- **Climate Change Advocates:** In the face of pressing global challenges like climate change, individuals advocating for environmental sustainability may emerge as silent catalysts, driving policy changes and international cooperation.

- **Technology and Governance Pioneers:** Innovators in emerging technologies, such as artificial intelligence and biotechnology, may become silent catalysts shaping the regulatory frameworks and ethical considerations of these fields.

11. Diplomacy Beyond State Boundaries:

- **Non-State Actors:** Silent catalysts are not confined to state actors. Non-state actors, including multinational corporations, NGOs, and influential individuals, can wield considerable influence on global policy, challenging traditional notions of state-centric diplomacy.

12. Lessons from History:

- **Unsung Heroes:** History is replete with unsung heroes whose contributions to global governance were overshadowed by more prominent figures. Recognizing and understanding the nuanced roles of these silent catalysts enriches our historical understanding.

13. Public Perception and Silent Catalysts:

- **Public Opinion Dynamics:** While silent catalysts may operate discreetly, public opinion dynamics can influence the latitude they have in shaping policies. Public support or opposition can amplify or impede their efforts.

14. Educational and Institutional Foundations:

- **Educational Initiatives:** The role of educational institutions in nurturing individuals who become silent catalysts is crucial. Educational initiatives fostering diplomatic skills, strategic thinking, and global awareness contribute to the development of future catalysts.

- **Think Tanks and Research Institutions:** Think tanks and research institutions play a role in incubating ideas and nurturing individuals who later become silent catalysts by contributing to policy development.

15. The Evolving Nature of Global Challenges:

- **Adaptability:** Silent catalysts must demonstrate adaptability in the face of evolving global challenges. The nature of contemporary issues, from pandemics to cybersecurity, requires individuals who can navigate complex, interconnected landscapes.

16. Unseen Contributions to Crisis Resolution:

- **Crisis Diplomacy:** Silent catalysts often play pivotal roles in crisis diplomacy. Their ability to discreetly navigate crises, mediate conflicts, and broker agreements contributes significantly to international stability.

17. Collective Action and Global Impact:

- **Networks of Influence:** Silent catalysts often operate within networks, and their collective action can lead to a more significant global impact. Cooperative efforts amplify their influence and contribute to the resolution of shared challenges.

18. The Legacy of Silent Catalysts:

- **Long-Term Impact:** The legacy of silent catalysts extends beyond their immediate contributions. Their influence shapes the trajectory of global governance, leaving a lasting imprint on policies, institutions, and the international order.

In conclusion, silent catalysts represent a dynamic and often unheralded force in the shaping of global policies. Whether operating within diplomatic circles, influencing cultural narratives, or driving technological innovations, these individuals navigate the complexities of international relations to leave an indelible mark on the course of human history. Understanding their roles, strategies, and the ethical dimensions of their actions is crucial for comprehending the intricate web of global governance and the unseen hands that guide its evolution.

CHAPTER 27: DARK DIPLOMACY: NAVIGATING THE UNDERBELLY OF INTERNATIONAL RELATIONS

Dark Diplomacy is an enigmatic realm within the broader scope of international relations, where clandestine maneuvers, covert operations, and unconventional strategies shape the landscape of global politics. This clandestine underbelly operates outside the public eye, often involving intelligence agencies, covert agents, and shadowy networks. To unravel the intricacies of Dark Diplomacy, it's essential to delve into its historical evolution, the actors involved, the covert methods employed, the ethical considerations, and the enduring impact on the geopolitics of nations.

1. Historical Evolution of Dark Diplomacy:

- **Cold War Espionage:** The Cold War era witnessed the height of Dark Diplomacy, with intelligence agencies such as the CIA (Central Intelligence Agency) and the KGB (Committee for State Security) engaging in covert operations, espionage, and subversion.

- **World Wars and Secret Operations:** Both World Wars saw the use of clandestine operations, including espionage and sabotage. The British Special Operations Executive (SOE) in World War II and its American counterpart, the Office of Strategic Services (OSS), exemplified the use of covert tactics.

2. Actors in Dark Diplomacy:

- **Intelligence Agencies:** National intelligence agencies, like the CIA, MI6, Mossad, and the FSB, play pivotal roles in Dark Diplomacy. They conduct covert operations to gather intelligence, influence foreign governments, and protect national interests.

- **Special Forces:** Military special forces, such as the United States Navy SEALs and the British SAS, are sometimes involved in covert operations, including targeted assassinations, hostage rescues, and unconventional warfare.

- **Non-State Actors:** Non-state entities, including private security firms and mercenaries, may be employed for covert operations. These actors operate in the shadows, serving the interests of governments or powerful individuals.

3. Covert Methods Employed:

- **Espionage:** Gathering classified information through espionage is a core element of Dark Diplomacy. Spies, often operating under deep cover, infiltrate foreign governments, organizations, or networks to extract sensitive information.

- **Sabotage and Subversion:** Covert operations may involve sabotaging critical infrastructure, disrupting communication networks, or subverting political processes to destabilize adversaries.

- **Assassinations and Targeted Killings:** The elimination of key individuals through targeted assassinations is a dark facet of covert operations. This method is used to eliminate perceived threats or destabilize rival regimes.

- **Propaganda and Disinformation:** Dark Diplomacy often employs propaganda and disinformation campaigns to manipulate public opinion, sow discord in rival nations, or influence electoral processes.

- **Cyber Warfare:** With the rise of technology, cyber warfare has become a prominent tool in Dark Diplomacy. Covert cyber-attacks aim to disrupt infrastructure, steal sensitive information, or conduct covert influence operations.

4. Ethical Considerations in Dark Diplomacy:

- **Legality and International Law:** Covert operations often operate in a legal gray area. The use of assassinations, covert interventions, and espionage raises ethical questions regarding compliance with international law and norms.

- **Accountability and Oversight:** Dark Diplomacy lacks transparency and oversight, leading to concerns about accountability. The absence of clear mechanisms for accountability raises ethical dilemmas regarding the use of covert methods.

- **Collateral Damage:** Covert operations can result in unintended consequences and collateral damage. Ethical considerations weigh the costs of achieving objectives against the potential harm to innocent civilians or non-combatants.

5. Enduring Impact on Geopolitics:

- **Destabilization of Regimes:** Covert interventions, such as supporting opposition groups or orchestrating coups, can lead to the destabilization of governments. This can have long-term consequences, shaping the geopolitical landscape of regions.

- **Creation of Proxy Wars:** Dark Diplomacy often involves the creation of proxy wars, where nations support surrogate forces to advance their interests without direct involvement. These conflicts have enduring impacts on global stability.

- **Intelligence Gathering:** The intelligence gathered through covert means contributes to a nation's understanding of global affairs. This information influences policy decisions, military strategies, and diplomatic initiatives.

6. Case Studies of Dark Diplomacy:

- **Operation Gladio:** A covert NATO operation during the Cold War, Operation Gladio involved the establishment of secret "stay-behind" armies in Europe to counter potential Soviet invasions. It operated in secrecy for decades and raised ethical questions about its impact on democracy.

- **Stuxnet Virus:** The Stuxnet virus, allegedly developed by the United States and Israel, was used to sabotage Iran's nuclear program. This cyber-attack demonstrated the use of covert methods in the realm of cyber warfare.

7. Espionage and Intelligence Gathering:

- **Signals Intelligence (SIGINT):** Dark Diplomacy heavily relies on signals intelligence, where intercepted communications, electronic surveillance, and code-breaking provide valuable information.

- **Human Intelligence (HUMINT):** Covert agents, known as spies, provide human intelligence by infiltrating organizations, governments, or networks. This method often involves significant risk and requires meticulous covert operations.

8. Technological Advancements in Dark Diplomacy:

- **Cyber Espionage:** The integration of technology has amplified the role of cyber espionage in Dark

Diplomacy. State-sponsored hacking, information warfare, and the use of malware have become prominent tools.

- **Surveillance Technologies:** Advanced surveillance technologies, including drones, facial recognition, and satellite imagery, enhance the capabilities of intelligence agencies engaged in covert operations.

9. Dark Diplomacy in the Information Age:

- **Disinformation Campaigns:** The Information Age has facilitated the spread of disinformation, enabling covert actors to manipulate public opinion through social media, online platforms, and misinformation campaigns.

- **Cyber Espionage and Information Warfare:** Dark Diplomacy in the Information Age involves sophisticated cyber-espionage campaigns targeting critical infrastructure, governments, and private entities.

10. The Role of Non-State Actors:

- **Private Military Companies (PMCs):** Non-state actors, particularly private military companies, are increasingly involved in covert operations. These entities operate with flexibility, sometimes blurring the lines between state and non-state actors.

- **Hacktivist Groups:** Non-state hacktivist groups, acting independently or in alignment with state interests, engage in cyber-attacks, information leaks, and online disruptions as part of Dark Diplomacy.

11. Countering Dark Diplomacy:

- **International Cooperation:** Countering Dark Diplomacy requires international cooperation and agreements that establish norms for acceptable behavior in cyberspace, intelligence gathering, and covert operations.

- **Strengthening Cybersecurity:** Nations must invest in robust cybersecurity measures to protect critical infrastructure and sensitive information from covert cyber-attacks.

- **Ethical Considerations:** Addressing the ethical considerations of Dark Diplomacy requires promoting transparency, accountability, and adherence to international legal norms in intelligence and covert operations.

12. Public Perception and Secrecy:

- **Public Distrust:** The secrecy inherent in Dark Diplomacy often leads to public distrust. The lack of transparency raises questions about the legitimacy of actions taken in the name of national security.

- **Media's Role:** The media plays a crucial role in shaping public perception of Dark Diplomacy. Investigative journalism and the uncovering of covert operations contribute to public awareness and scrutiny.

13. Shaping Future Geopolitics:

- **Evolution of Covert Methods:** Dark Diplomacy will continue to evolve with advancements in technology and changes in global power dynamics. The development of new covert methods, both in the physical and cyber domains, will shape the future of geopolitics.

- **Shifts in Alliances:** Covert actions can lead to shifts in alliances and international relations. The geopolitical landscape will be influenced by the clandestine efforts of nations to advance their interests.

14. The Moral Quandary of Dark Diplomacy:

- **Ethics and Morality:** Dark Diplomacy raises profound ethical questions about the morality of covert actions. Balancing national interests with ethical considerations remains a persistent challenge for those involved in clandestine operations.

15. Unintended Consequences:

- **Blowback:** Covert interventions can result in unintended consequences, leading to blowback where actions intended to serve national interests inadvertently create long-term challenges and conflicts.

16. Lessons from History:

- **Mistakes and Learnings:** Examining historical instances of Dark Diplomacy provides valuable lessons. Understanding the mistakes and unintended consequences of covert actions can inform future diplomatic strategies.

17. The Human Element in Dark Diplomacy:

- **Agent Recruitment and Handling:** The recruitment and handling of agents remain central to Dark Diplomacy. The human element introduces a dynamic and unpredictable factor in covert operations.

18. The Nexus of Dark Diplomacy and Traditional Diplomacy:

- **Interplay between Dark and Traditional Diplomacy:** Dark Diplomacy and traditional diplomacy are interconnected, with covert actions sometimes complementing or conflicting with overt diplomatic efforts. Understanding this interplay is essential for a comprehensive approach to international relations.

In conclusion, Dark Diplomacy operates in the shadows, exerting influence, shaping outcomes, and contributing to the intricate dance of international relations. It raises ethical questions, demands careful scrutiny, and underscores the complex and multifaceted nature of global politics. As technology advances and the geopolitical landscape evolves, the role of Dark Diplomacy will continue to be a critical factor in the shaping of the world order, highlighting the need for vigilance, accountability, and a nuanced understanding of the forces at play in the underbelly of international relations.

CHAPTER 28: THE SILK ROAD REDUX: ECONOMIC GEOPOLITICS IN THE 21ST CENTURY

The Silk Road, once a historic network of trade routes connecting the East and West, has found a modern revival in the 21st century, not as a physical pathway of caravans and camels, but as a complex web of economic geopolitics. In this contemporary landscape, nations are engaged in a new Silk Road Redux, driven by economic imperatives, infrastructure projects, and geopolitical maneuvering. Understanding the dynamics of this revived Silk Road involves exploring the historical context, key players, economic initiatives, strategic implications, challenges faced, and the transformative impact on global economic geopolitics.

1. Historical Context:

- **Ancient Silk Road:** The ancient Silk Road facilitated the exchange of goods, culture, and ideas between Asia, Europe, and Africa. It played a pivotal role in shaping civilizations and fostering economic interdependence.

- **Revival in the 21st Century:** The Silk Road Redux refers to contemporary initiatives that echo the historical Silk Road's spirit, emphasizing connectivity, trade, and economic cooperation across regions.

2. Key Players in the Silk Road Redux:

- **China's Belt and Road Initiative (BRI):** Spearheaded by China, the Belt and Road Initiative is a colossal infrastructure project encompassing land-based Silk Road Economic Belt and the 21st Century Maritime Silk Road. It aims to connect Asia with Europe and

Africa through a network of railways, highways, ports, and other infrastructure.

- **Central Asian Nations:** Nations in Central Asia, including Kazakhstan, Uzbekistan, and Turkmenistan, play crucial roles in the Silk Road Redux due to their strategic geographical locations and historical ties to the ancient Silk Road.

- **European Countries:** European nations, particularly those in Eastern Europe, are integral players as they seek to benefit from enhanced trade links and infrastructure development facilitated by the Silk Road Redux.

- **Middle Eastern Countries:** Countries in the Middle East, such as Iran and the Gulf States, are positioned as vital hubs in the Silk Road Redux, linking Asia to Europe and fostering economic ties.

3. Economic Initiatives and Projects:

- **Belt and Road Initiative (BRI):** Launched in 2013, the BRI is the flagship economic initiative of the Silk Road Redux. It includes a vast network of infrastructure projects, including railways, highways, ports, and energy pipelines, aimed at fostering economic integration and development across participating nations.

- **Digital Silk Road:** Beyond physical infrastructure, the Silk Road Redux includes the Digital Silk Road, focusing on digital connectivity, e-commerce, and technology collaborations to enhance economic ties among participating nations.

- **China-Pakistan Economic Corridor (CPEC):** A subset of the BRI, the CPEC is a notable infrastructure project linking Gwadar Port in Pakistan to China's northwestern region. It exemplifies the economic and strategic dimensions of the Silk Road Redux.

4. Strategic Implications of the Silk Road Redux:

- **Geopolitical Influence:** The Silk Road Redux provides nations, particularly China, with an avenue to expand geopolitical influence by fostering economic dependencies and partnerships along the trade routes.

- **Economic Diplomacy:** The initiative promotes economic diplomacy, allowing nations to leverage economic ties for political influence and regional stability.

- **Shifts in Global Trade Routes:** The Silk Road Redux has the potential to alter global trade routes, reducing dependence on traditional maritime routes and creating new pathways for goods and services.

5. Challenges Faced by the Silk Road Redux:

- **Debt Sustainability:** Concerns have been raised about the debt sustainability of nations participating in the BRI, particularly smaller economies that may struggle to repay loans for infrastructure projects.

- **Security Concerns:** Geopolitical tensions, regional conflicts, and security challenges along the Silk Road Redux pose risks to the smooth implementation of infrastructure projects and economic activities.

- **Environmental Impact:** Large-scale infrastructure projects can have significant environmental consequences, raising concerns about the ecological sustainability of the Silk Road Redux.

6. Transformative Impact on Global Economic Geopolitics:

- **Economic Reshaping:** The Silk Road Redux is reshaping the global economic landscape by creating new economic corridors, fostering trade, and enhancing economic cooperation among nations.

- **Emerging Markets and Connectivity:** The initiative facilitates connectivity between emerging markets, promoting economic growth, and providing new opportunities for businesses across diverse sectors.

- **Diversification of Trade Routes:** Nations are increasingly diversifying their trade routes, reducing dependence on traditional maritime routes and creating alternative pathways for the transportation of goods.

7. Cultural Exchange and Soft Power:

- **Cultural Diplomacy:** The Silk Road Redux fosters cultural exchange by reconnecting regions with shared histories and promoting understanding among diverse civilizations.

- **Soft Power Projection:** Participating nations, especially China, utilize the Silk Road Redux as a means of projecting soft power by showcasing cultural heritage, fostering people-to-people exchanges, and promoting mutual understanding.

8. Technological Advancements in the Silk Road Redux:

- **Digital Connectivity:** Technological advancements, including 5G networks and digital infrastructure, play a pivotal role in the Silk Road Redux. Digital connectivity enhances communication, e-commerce, and technology collaborations among participating nations.

- **Smart Cities and Innovation Hubs:** Some Silk Road

Redux projects include the development of smart cities and innovation hubs, contributing to technological advancements and economic innovation.

9. Social and Economic Inclusivity:

- **Poverty Alleviation:** The Silk Road Redux has the potential to contribute to poverty alleviation by fostering economic development in participating regions and creating job opportunities.

- **Inclusive Growth:** Inclusive economic growth is a goal of the initiative, aiming to benefit a broad spectrum of society by reducing economic disparities and promoting shared prosperity.

10. Environmental Considerations and Sustainability:

- **Green Initiatives:** Some projects within the Silk Road Redux incorporate green initiatives and sustainable development practices to mitigate environmental impact and address climate change concerns.

- **Eco-friendly Infrastructure:** Developing eco-friendly and sustainable infrastructure is a focus, reflecting an awareness of the environmental challenges associated with large-scale development projects.

11. Economic Cooperation Beyond Borders:

- **Cross-Border Economic Zones:** The Silk Road Redux fosters the creation of cross-border economic zones, encouraging economic cooperation beyond traditional national boundaries.

- **Trade Facilitation:** Efforts to simplify customs procedures, reduce trade barriers, and enhance logistical efficiency contribute to the facilitation of cross-border trade.

12. Legal Frameworks and Governance:

- **International Legal Frameworks:** The Silk Road Redux requires robust international legal frameworks to govern cross-border trade, resolve disputes, and ensure the fair and transparent implementation of projects.

- **Governance Mechanisms:** Effective governance mechanisms are essential to address challenges, ensure accountability, and facilitate cooperation among participating nations.

13. Lessons from the Ancient Silk Road:

- **Cultural Harmony:** The historical Silk Road was characterized by cultural harmony and exchange. Lessons from this era highlight the importance of fostering cultural understanding and collaboration in the contemporary Silk Road Redux.

- **Mutual Economic Benefits:** The success of the ancient Silk Road was rooted in the mutual economic benefits derived from trade. This principle remains relevant in the modern Silk Road Redux.

14. The Role of Multilateral Institutions:

- **Involvement of International Organizations:** Multilateral institutions, such as the Asian Infrastructure Investment Bank (AIIB) and the World Bank, play roles in financing and overseeing projects within the Silk Road Redux, adding an element of international collaboration.

15. Geostrategic Significance of Key Nodes:

- **Strategic Ports:** Ports along the Maritime Silk Road, including Gwadar in Pakistan and Piraeus in Greece, gain geostrategic significance, acting as key nodes for trade and economic connectivity.

- **Transportation Hubs:** Transportation hubs, such as those in Central Asia and the Middle East, become crucial nodes connecting different segments of the Silk Road Redux.

16. Economic Corridors and Regional Integration:

- **Economic Corridors:** The development of economic corridors, such as the China-Pakistan Economic Corridor, promotes regional integration by connecting economies and fostering cross-border economic cooperation.

- **Influence on Regional Organizations:** The Silk Road Redux influences regional organizations, encouraging them to collaborate on economic development and infrastructure projects for mutual benefit.

17. Future Trajectories of the Silk Road Redux:

- **Expansion and Evolution:** The Silk Road Redux is likely to expand and evolve, with new projects, collaborations, and technological advancements shaping its trajectory.

- **Integration with Global Economic Trends:** The initiative will likely integrate with broader global economic trends, including the rise of digital economies, sustainable development goals, and the shifting dynamics of international trade.

18. Mitigating Risks and Challenges:

- **Risk Management Strategies:** To ensure the success of the Silk Road Redux, nations and stakeholders must implement effective risk management strategies, addressing concerns related to debt sustainability, security, and environmental impact.

- **Transparent Communication:** Transparent communication and cooperation among participating nations are essential to address geopolitical tensions and ensure a collaborative approach to economic development.

In conclusion, the Silk Road Redux represents a paradigm shift in global economic geopolitics, where nations are intricately linked by a network of infrastructure projects, trade routes, and technological collaborations. This economic revival carries the legacy of the ancient Silk Road into the 21st century, fostering connectivity, cultural exchange, and economic cooperation. As the initiative continues to unfold, its impact on global economic dynamics, geopolitical relationships, and the shared prosperity of participating nations will shape the course of international relations in the years to come.

CHAPTER 29: SILENT WATCHERS: NON-STATE ACTORS IN GLOBAL AFFAIRS

In the complex tapestry of global affairs, non-state actors have emerged as influential entities that transcend traditional geopolitical boundaries. These Silent Watchers, ranging from multinational corporations and non-governmental organizations to transnational criminal networks and influential individuals, play pivotal roles in shaping the course of international relations. This comprehensive exploration delves into the historical context, typology of non-state actors, their modes of influence, the impact on global governance, ethical considerations, and the evolving landscape of their roles in contemporary global affairs.

1. Historical Context:

- **Emergence of Non-State Actors**: Throughout history, non-state actors have played roles in shaping global affairs, from the powerful merchant guilds of medieval Europe to religious institutions that exerted considerable influence during various historical periods.

- **Acceleration in the 20th Century**: The 20th century witnessed an acceleration of non-state actor influence, with the rise of multinational corporations, advocacy groups, and global networks that operate beyond the confines of traditional state-centric diplomacy.

2. Typology of Non-State Actors:

- **Multinational Corporations (MNCs):** Global corporations wield immense economic power, influencing governments, shaping trade policies, and often transcending the regulatory capacity of individual nations.

- **Non-Governmental Organizations (NGOs):** NGOs, ranging from humanitarian groups to advocacy organizations, contribute to global governance by addressing issues such as human rights, environmental protection, and public health.

- **Transnational Criminal Networks:** Illicit organizations, such as drug cartels and human trafficking networks, operate across borders, challenging the sovereignty of nation-states and posing complex security threats.

- **International Organizations:** Bodies like the United Nations (UN), World Bank, and International Monetary Fund (IMF) function as non-state actors, providing platforms for global cooperation and governance.

- **Influential Individuals:** High-net-worth individuals, philanthropists, and influential personalities play direct roles in shaping global affairs through their financial contributions, advocacy, and strategic influence.

3. Modes of Influence:

- **Economic Power:** Multinational corporations leverage economic power to influence policies, trade agreements, and even impact the domestic politics of nations.

- **Soft Power and Advocacy:** NGOs exert influence through soft power, shaping public opinion, advocating for policy changes, and influencing international norms and standards.

- **Cyber Capabilities:** Non-state actors, including hacktivist groups and cybercriminal organizations, leverage technology to disrupt systems, steal sensitive information, and influence political narratives.

- **Philanthropy and Public-Private Partnerships:** Foundations and wealthy individuals contribute to global affairs through philanthropy, funding initiatives related to education, public health, and sustainable development.

- **Networks and Alliances:** Transnational criminal networks form alliances, creating complex webs that challenge traditional law enforcement and security measures.

4. Impact on Global Governance:

- **Supranational Governance Structures:** Non-state actors contribute to the evolution of supranational governance structures, challenging the conventional Westphalian model and fostering a more interconnected global system.

- **Policy Advocacy and Implementation:** NGOs play vital roles in policy advocacy, implementation, and monitoring, holding states accountable for their commitments in areas such as human rights, environmental protection, and social justice.

- **Economic Integration:** Multinational corporations drive economic integration, influencing trade policies, investment patterns, and the redistribution of wealth on a global scale.

- **Humanitarian Interventions:** NGOs and international organizations often take the lead in humanitarian interventions, responding to crises, providing aid, and addressing issues like refugee displacement and natural disasters.

5. Ethical Considerations:

- **Accountability and Transparency:** The lack of democratic accountability and transparency in the operations of some non-state actors raises ethical concerns. Balancing their influence with accountability mechanisms becomes crucial.

- **Human Rights Impact:** Non-state actors, particularly corporations operating in regions with weak regulatory frameworks, can impact human rights, labor conditions, and environmental standards. Ethical considerations involve mitigating negative consequences and promoting responsible business practices.

- **Power Disparities:** The power disparities between non-state actors and individual nations or marginalized communities highlight ethical dilemmas. Ensuring that the influence of non-state actors aligns with broader ethical principles becomes imperative.

6. Evolving Landscape of Non-State Actors:

- **Digital Activism:** Non-state actors leverage digital platforms for activism, mobilization, and advocacy, demonstrating the evolving role of technology in shaping global affairs.

- **Climate Activism:** Environmental NGOs and grassroots movements play increasingly influential roles in shaping global climate policies, advocating for sustainable practices, and holding both state and non-state actors accountable for their environmental impact.

- **Global Health Initiatives:** NGOs and philanthropic foundations contribute significantly to global health initiatives, addressing issues such as pandemics, access to healthcare, and medical research.

- **Hybrid Warfare:** Non-state actors engage in hybrid warfare, combining conventional and unconventional tactics, including cyber-attacks, disinformation campaigns, and proxy conflicts, to achieve strategic objectives.

7. Challenges Faced by Non-State Actors:

- **Regulatory Challenges:** Non-state actors often face challenges related to inconsistent regulations across nations, creating legal ambiguities and potential conflicts.

- **Security Risks:** NGOs and corporations operating in conflict zones face security risks, with potential repercussions for their personnel and operations.

- **Ethical Dilemmas:** Non-state actors grapple with ethical dilemmas, especially when their activities intersect with sensitive geopolitical issues or when they inadvertently contribute to negative consequences.

8. Influence in Crisis and Conflict:

- **Humanitarian Interventions:** NGOs often play key roles in humanitarian interventions during conflicts, providing aid, protection, and advocacy for vulnerable populations.

- **Conflict Resolution:** Non-state actors may contribute to conflict resolution efforts, acting as mediators, facilitators, or sources of diplomatic pressure.

9. Collaborative Initiatives:

- **Public-Private Partnerships:** Collaborative initiatives involving both state and non-state actors, such as public-private partnerships, contribute to addressing complex global challenges, including infrastructure development, healthcare, and education.

- **Multi-Stakeholder Forums:** Platforms that bring together governments, businesses, NGOs, and other stakeholders foster collaboration, allowing for comprehensive and inclusive approaches to problem-solving.

10. Cultural and Social Impact:

- **Cultural Diplomacy:** Non-state actors contribute to cultural diplomacy by fostering exchanges, collaborations, and initiatives that promote understanding and appreciation of diverse cultures.

- **Social Movements:** Grassroots movements and civil society organizations shape social narratives, challenge injustices, and contribute to societal transformations.

11. Geoeconomic Dimensions:

- **Investment and Economic Diplomacy:** Multinational corporations engage in geoeconomic strategies, aligning their investments with geopolitical objectives and influencing the economic policies of host nations.

- **Global Supply Chains:** Non-state actors play pivotal roles in global supply chains, influencing production, distribution, and consumption patterns on a global scale.

12. The Role of Media and Information Dissemination:

- **Media as Non-State Actors:** Media organizations, as non-state actors, influence public opinion, shape narratives, and contribute to the dissemination of information that can impact geopolitical dynamics.

- **Disinformation Challenges:** Non-state actors, including hacktivist groups and state-sponsored entities, engage in disinformation campaigns, posing challenges to the reliability of information and international discourse.

13. Future Trends and Challenges:

- **Technological Advancements:** The continued integration of advanced technologies, including artificial intelligence, blockchain, and biotechnology, will shape the roles and capabilities of non-state actors in unforeseen ways.

- **Global Governance Reforms:** The influence of non-state actors may drive calls for reforms in global governance structures to better address contemporary challenges and ensure more inclusive decision-making processes.

14. Balancing Non-State Actor Influence:

- **Normative Frameworks:** Developing normative frameworks and international agreements that govern the conduct of non-state actors become essential to balance their influence and uphold ethical standards.

- **Enhancing State Capacities:** Strengthening the capacities of states to regulate, collaborate, and negotiate with non-state actors is crucial for maintaining a balance of power and ensuring the primacy of state sovereignty.

15. Case Studies:

- **Global Impact of NGOs:** Organizations like Amnesty International and Médecins Sans Frontières serve as examples of NGOs with significant global impacts, influencing human rights standards and providing critical humanitarian aid.

- **Corporate Social Responsibility:** Examining corporate initiatives, such as the sustainability efforts of companies like Unilever or the environmental commitments of tech giants, highlights the evolving role of corporations in global affairs.

16. Education and Advocacy:

- **Educational Initiatives:** Non-state actors contribute to global affairs through educational initiatives that promote awareness, critical thinking, and cross-cultural understanding.

- **Advocacy for Global Causes:** NGOs and advocacy groups champion global causes, pushing for policy changes, addressing social issues, and promoting justice on an international scale.

17. Theoretical Frameworks:

- **Constructivism:** The constructivist approach highlights how non-state actors contribute to shaping global norms, identities, and the very structure of international relations.

- **Liberal Institutionalism:** Liberal institutionalism emphasizes the role of international institutions, where non-state actors often participate, in fostering cooperation and managing global challenges.

18. Conclusion: In the silent corridors of global affairs, non-state actors emerge as influential forces, shaping the destiny of nations, policies, and the well-being of humanity. As these Silent Watchers continue to evolve, their roles, impacts, and ethical considerations will remain integral components of the ever-changing landscape of international relations. Understanding their dynamics becomes paramount for crafting effective global governance mechanisms, fostering cooperation, and navigating the complex web of interests and influences that define our interconnected world.

CHAPTER 30: GEOECONOMICS: THE SILENT POWER PLAY

In the realm of international relations, the term "geoeconomics" has emerged as a powerful concept, signifying the intersection of economic policies and geopolitical strategies employed by nations to achieve their national interests. Unlike traditional warfare or overt geopolitical maneuvers, geoeconomics represents a subtle yet impactful form of power play. This detailed exploration delves into the historical roots, key components, strategic implications, tools utilized, ethical considerations, and the evolving nature of geoeconomics as a silent force shaping the global order.

1. Historical Roots:

- **Mercantilism and Colonialism:** The historical roots of geoeconomics trace back to mercantilist practices during the age of colonialism. Nations sought economic dominance through control over resources, trade routes, and colonies.

- **Cold War Era:** The Cold War era witnessed the use of economic tools as instruments of geopolitical influence. The United States and the Soviet Union engaged in economic aid, trade incentives, and sanctions to shape the geopolitical landscape.

2. Key Components of Geoeconomics:

- **Trade and Investment Policies:** Nations leverage trade agreements, tariffs, and investment policies to advance their geopolitical objectives, promoting economic ties with allies and imposing restrictions on adversaries.

- **Financial Instruments:** The use of financial

instruments, such as sanctions, asset freezes, and financial aid, constitutes a key component of geoeconomic strategies.

- **Technological Dominance:** The pursuit of technological leadership and control over critical technologies serves as a means to enhance geopolitical influence in the modern era.

- **Energy Policies:** Control over energy resources and the manipulation of energy markets are integral components, allowing nations to influence global energy security and exert leverage over energy-dependent states.

- **Infrastructure Projects:** Geoeconomics involves the implementation of strategic infrastructure projects to enhance connectivity, foster economic dependence, and extend geopolitical influence.

3. Strategic Implications of Geoeconomics:

- **Power Projection:** Geoeconomics serves as a means of power projection, enabling nations to extend influence without resorting to military interventions. Economic dominance becomes a key determinant of geopolitical standing.

- **Regional Hegemony:** Geoeconomic strategies contribute to the establishment of regional hegemony, allowing nations to shape the economic and political landscape within their spheres of influence.

- **Alliance Building:** Nations engage in geoeconomic practices to build alliances, cultivate economic partnerships, and create dependencies that align with their geopolitical goals.

- **Deterrence and Coercion:** Geoeconomic tools, such

as sanctions or trade restrictions, are employed for deterrence and coercion, compelling nations to conform to desired geopolitical behaviors.

4. Tools Utilized in Geoeconomics:

- **Sanctions:** Economic sanctions, including trade restrictions and asset freezes, are employed to coerce or penalize nations for geopolitical actions contrary to the interests of the enforcing state.

- **Investment Diplomacy:** Nations strategically use investments, foreign aid, and development projects to enhance their geopolitical influence, particularly in developing regions.

- **Technology Controls:** The control and manipulation of critical technologies, such as semiconductors and artificial intelligence, serve as tools to establish technological dominance and exert influence.

- **Currency Manipulation:** The manipulation of currencies, including devaluation or exchange rate policies, is employed to gain economic advantages and influence trade balances.

- **Bilateral and Regional Trade Agreements:** Nations engage in negotiations for bilateral and regional trade agreements, using economic partnerships to solidify geopolitical alignments and create spheres of influence.

- **Debt Diplomacy:** The strategic use of loans and financial aid is employed to create economic dependencies, influencing the policies and decision-making of debtor nations.

5. Ethical Considerations in Geoeconomics:

- **Humanitarian Impact:** Geoeconomic strategies,

particularly sanctions, can have severe humanitarian consequences, impacting the livelihoods and well-being of ordinary citizens in targeted nations.

- **Environmental Concerns:** Pursuit of economic interests in geoeconomics may lead to environmental exploitation and degradation, raising ethical questions about sustainability.

- **Labor Practices:** Nations engaging in geoeconomic competition might overlook or tolerate poor labor practices in pursuit of economic advantage, posing ethical dilemmas.

6. Evolving Nature of Geoeconomics:

- **Technology and Digital Economy:** The digital economy and technological advancements have added new dimensions to geoeconomics, with data governance, cybersecurity, and control over emerging technologies becoming critical components.

- **Climate Change and Resource Competition:** As concerns over climate change rise, geoeconomics intersects with resource competition, shaping strategies related to renewable energy, resource extraction, and environmental conservation.

- **Pandemic Response:** The global response to pandemics introduces new considerations, with geoeconomic strategies influencing vaccine distribution, medical supply chains, and international cooperation.

7. Global Players in Geoeconomics:

- **China's Belt and Road Initiative (BRI):** China's BRI is a prime example of geoeconomic strategy, involving massive infrastructure projects that enhance economic connectivity and extend geopolitical influence.

- **United States Economic Statecraft:** The United States employs economic statecraft, utilizing sanctions, trade policies, and investment incentives to advance its geopolitical objectives.

- **European Union (EU):** The EU engages in geoeconomic strategies through trade agreements, regulatory frameworks, and development aid, shaping its influence in neighboring regions.

8. Challenges Faced by Geoeconomics:

- **Multilateral Cooperation:** Achieving geoeconomic goals often requires multilateral cooperation. Challenges arise when nations pursue unilateral strategies that may lead to global tensions.

- **Unintended Consequences:** Geoeconomic actions can have unintended consequences, affecting global markets, regional stability, and relationships with other nations.

- **Resistance from Targeted Nations:** Nations targeted by geoeconomic measures may resist, developing counter-strategies and seeking alternative alliances to mitigate the impact.

9. Geoeconomics in the Digital Age:

- **Cybersecurity Challenges:** Geoeconomic strategies increasingly involve cyber capabilities, leading to challenges in cybersecurity and the protection of critical digital infrastructure.

- **Data Governance:** The governance of data, including issues of privacy, intellectual property, and data localization, becomes a crucial aspect of geoeconomic considerations in the digital age.

10. Economic Statecraft in Diplomacy:

- **Diplomatic Instruments:** Economic statecraft serves as a key instrument in diplomatic endeavors, influencing negotiations, peace processes, and the resolution of international conflicts.

- **Soft Power Projection:** Economic prowess enhances a nation's soft power, shaping global perceptions and fostering cultural influence.

11. Future Trends in Geoeconomics:

- **Green Geoeconomics:** The growing emphasis on sustainability and climate change mitigation is likely to influence geoeconomic strategies, with nations prioritizing green technologies and environmentally conscious practices.

- **Technological Innovation:** Ongoing technological innovations, including advancements in artificial intelligence, quantum computing, and biotechnology, will become central to geoeconomic competition.

- **Global Health Security:** The lessons learned from global health crises will impact geoeconomic strategies, influencing international collaboration in healthcare, vaccine development, and pandemic preparedness.

12. Global Governance Challenges:

- **Role of International Institutions:** The role of international institutions in governing geoeconomic practices and resolving disputes becomes increasingly important to ensure stability and prevent conflicts.

- **Normative Frameworks:** Developing normative frameworks and ethical guidelines for geoeconomic behavior is essential for fostering responsible practices and preventing abuse.

13. Public Perception and Geoeconomics:

- **Media Influence:** Media plays a crucial role in shaping public perception of geoeconomic actions. The narrative surrounding sanctions, trade policies, and economic statecraft influences public opinion and diplomatic outcomes.

- **Citizen Activism:** Public awareness and activism can impact geoeconomic strategies, with citizens advocating for ethical considerations, environmental sustainability, and humanitarian concerns.

14. Balancing Economic and Security Interests:

- **Trade-Offs and Compromises:** Nations must navigate the delicate balance between economic interests and national security concerns, making trade-offs and compromises to maintain geopolitical stability.

- **Long-Term Strategic Planning:** Successful geoeconomic strategies require long-term planning, considering the evolving global landscape, technological advancements, and geopolitical shifts.

15. Case Studies:

- **Russia's Energy Leverage:** Russia's use of its energy resources, particularly natural gas, as a geopolitical tool exemplifies the geoeconomic strategy of leveraging key assets for geopolitical influence.

- **U.S.-China Trade Relations:** The ongoing trade tensions between the United States and China showcase the complex interplay of geoeconomics, technology competition, and strategic rivalry.

16. Geoeconomics and Global Resilience:

- **Pandemic Resilience:** Geoeconomic strategies are central to building global resilience in the face of pandemics, influencing vaccine distribution, healthcare infrastructure, and international cooperation.

- **Economic Recovery:** Geoeconomic considerations shape post-pandemic economic recovery efforts, influencing stimulus packages, trade policies, and infrastructure investments.

17. Education and Awareness:

- **Public Diplomacy:** Nations engage in public diplomacy to educate global audiences about their geoeconomic policies, fostering understanding and countering negative perceptions.

- **Academic Research:** Academic institutions play a role in researching and analyzing geoeconomic strategies, providing insights that contribute to informed policy decisions.

18. Conclusion: Geoeconomics, as a silent power play, continues to redefine the contours of international relations. From historical precedents to contemporary complexities in the digital age, the fusion of economic instruments with geopolitical strategies has become a defining feature of global affairs. The ethical considerations, evolving trends, and the delicate balance required in navigating this silent power play underscore its significance in shaping the future geopolitical landscape. As nations grapple with the challenges and opportunities presented by geoeconomics, understanding its multifaceted nature becomes imperative for policymakers, diplomats, and citizens alike, ensuring a nuanced approach to the complex interplay between economic forces and global politics.

CHAPTER 31: SILENT BORDERS: REDEFINING NATIONAL BOUNDARIES

In the landscape of international relations, the concept of "Silent Borders" has emerged as a transformative force, challenging traditional notions of national boundaries and reshaping the dynamics of global governance. This exploration delves into the historical evolution of borders, the contemporary factors influencing their redefinition, the role of technology, legal implications, economic considerations, and the broader impact on identity, sovereignty, and geopolitics.

1. Historical Evolution of Borders:

- **Feudal and Agrarian Societies:** In agrarian and feudal societies, borders were often fluid, determined by natural features, local agreements, and the influence of regional powers.

- **Westphalian System:** The Peace of Westphalia in 1648 established the modern state system, formalizing the concept of fixed borders and state sovereignty.

- **Colonial Legacies:** Colonial powers drew artificial borders, often disregarding ethnic, linguistic, and cultural realities, leading to contemporary challenges in regions like Africa and the Middle East.

2. Factors Influencing Redefinition:

- **Globalization:** The interconnectedness of economies and the flow of information challenge the traditional role of borders in regulating trade, communication, and cultural exchange.

- **Technological Advances:** The digital age, with advancements in telecommunications, the internet, and blockchain, facilitates virtual interactions, blurring the physical constraints imposed by borders.

- **Migration and Diaspora:** Increasing global migration and the rise of diaspora communities contribute to a transnational identity, transcending traditional notions of belonging tied to a specific geographical space.

3. Technology and Virtual Borders:

- **Blockchain and Smart Contracts:** Blockchain technology enables the creation of secure, transparent, and decentralized systems, offering new possibilities for managing and recording cross-border transactions.

- **Virtual Identities:** The rise of virtual identities and online communities challenges the significance of physical borders in defining individual affiliations and allegiances.

- **Digital Currencies:** The emergence of digital currencies, like cryptocurrencies, introduces new means of conducting financial transactions that operate independently of traditional banking and national currencies.

4. Legal Implications:

- **International Law Challenges:** The redefinition of borders poses challenges to traditional international legal frameworks, as concepts of sovereignty and territorial integrity are reconsidered.

- **Human Rights and Citizenship:** Evolving notions of citizenship and human rights raise questions about the rights and protections afforded to individuals living in areas with shifting or contested borders.

5. Economic Considerations:

- **Global Supply Chains:** Economic globalization has led to the integration of global supply chains, rendering traditional borders less significant in the movement of goods and services.

- **Special Economic Zones:** Special Economic Zones (SEZs) and economic integration agreements challenge the traditional understanding of borders as barriers to trade, encouraging economic collaboration across borders.

6. Identity and Cultural Impact:

- **Transnational Identities:** The rise of transnational identities, shaped by migration, cultural exchange, and digital connectivity, challenges the notion that one's identity is strictly tied to a specific national territory.

- **Cultural Hybridization:** Increased interaction across borders results in cultural hybridization, blurring distinctions and enriching societies with diverse influences.

7. Regional Integration Initiatives:

- **European Union (EU):** The EU exemplifies a regional integration model where member states share open borders, fostering economic collaboration and free movement of people.

- **African Union (AU):** Efforts within the African Union aim at regional integration, seeking to overcome colonial-era borders for economic and political cooperation.

8. Security and Geopolitical Considerations:

- **Border Security Challenges:** Traditional notions of border security face challenges in the age of globalization, where non-state actors operate across borders, necessitating new approaches to security.

- **Cybersecurity Concerns:** The virtual realm poses new challenges, with cyber threats transcending physical borders and requiring international collaboration for effective security measures.

9. Challenges to Silent Borders:

- **Nationalism and Populism:** Resurgent nationalism and populism in some regions challenge the idea of open and flexible borders, emphasizing the need for strict territorial control.

- **Disputes Over Territorial Integrity:** Disputes over territorial integrity, exemplified by conflicts in regions like Crimea and Kashmir, highlight the enduring significance of physical borders.

10. Environmental Considerations:

- **Climate Change Impact:** Environmental challenges, such as climate change, can lead to the displacement of populations, prompting the need for international cooperation and reevaluation of traditional border policies.

- **Shared Resources:** Management of shared resources, such as water bodies and forests, requires collaborative efforts that go beyond rigid national borders.

11. Case Studies:

- **Schengen Agreement:** The Schengen Agreement in Europe, allowing for passport-free travel across participating countries, illustrates the practical implementation of open borders within a regional context.

- **Northern Triangle Migration:** The migration challenges in the

Northern Triangle of Central America highlight the complex interplay of socioeconomic factors, security concerns, and national borders.

12. Diplomatic and Multilateral Approaches:

- **Diplomacy in Border Disputes:** Diplomatic efforts play a crucial role in resolving border disputes, emphasizing dialogue, negotiation, and mutual understanding.

- **Role of International Organizations:** Bodies like the United Nations and regional organizations mediate conflicts, promote cooperation, and address the challenges posed by shifting borders.

13. Public Opinion and Societal Perceptions:

- **Public Perception of Borders:** Societal attitudes toward borders vary, with some embracing the idea of open borders for economic and cultural exchange, while others emphasize the need for strict controls for security reasons.

- **Media Influence:** Media shapes public perceptions of borders, influencing narratives on immigration, security, and the impact of globalization.

14. Ethical Considerations:

- **Humanitarian Concerns:** Ethical considerations arise in the context of humanitarian challenges, such as refugee crises, where the rigid enforcement of borders can lead to human suffering.

- **Cultural Preservation:** Ethical questions surround the preservation of cultural diversity, as open borders may contribute to cultural homogenization or exploitation.

15. Future Trends and Predictions:

- **Digital Citizenship:** The concept of digital citizenship may gain prominence, emphasizing rights and responsibilities in the virtual realm, transcending traditional national boundaries.

- **Evolving Geopolitical Alignments:** Changing geopolitical dynamics, influenced by economic interests and technological advancements, will continue to impact the redefinition of borders.

16. Educational Initiatives:

- **Global Citizenship Education:** Educational initiatives that promote global citizenship can foster an understanding of interconnectedness, encouraging individuals to transcend traditional notions of national identity.

17. Conclusion: The concept of Silent Borders challenges the static nature of traditional national boundaries, reflecting the dynamic forces of globalization, technology, and changing geopolitical realities. As the world navigates these transformations, policymakers, diplomats, and citizens grapple with the ethical, legal, and geopolitical implications of redefining borders. Whether through regional integration, technological advancements, or diplomatic endeavors, the evolution of borders remains a complex and evolving aspect of international relations. Understanding and navigating this paradigm shift requires a nuanced approach that balances the needs of security, identity, and cooperation in the ever-changing landscape of global governance.

CHAPTER 32: ENERGY DIPLOMACY: POWER PLAYS IN THE RESOURCE LANDSCAPE

Energy Diplomacy represents a strategic intersection of international relations and global energy dynamics. As the world grapples with the increasing demand for energy, nations engage in complex geopolitical maneuvers to secure access to resources, ensure energy security, and leverage their positions on the global stage. This exploration delves into the historical context, key players, geopolitical considerations, technological advancements, environmental implications, and the evolving landscape of Energy Diplomacy.

1. Historical Context:

- **Colonial Resource Exploitation:** Historical energy diplomacy traces back to the colonial era when major powers sought control over resource-rich territories for their energy needs.

- **Oil and Geopolitics:** The 20th century witnessed the emergence of oil as a critical energy resource, leading to geopolitical struggles and the establishment of oil diplomacy as a key component of international relations.

2. Key Players in Global Energy Diplomacy:

- **Major Energy Producers:** Nations with significant energy reserves, such as Russia, Saudi Arabia, and the United States, play central roles in shaping global energy dynamics.

- **Consuming Nations:** Energy-consuming nations,

including China, the European Union, and India, engage in diplomacy to secure reliable energy sources and diversify their energy portfolios.

- **International Organizations:** Entities like OPEC (Organization of the Petroleum Exporting Countries) and the International Energy Agency (IEA) influence global energy diplomacy through market regulations, data sharing, and policy coordination.

3. Geopolitical Considerations:

- **Pipeline Politics:** The construction of energy pipelines, such as the Nord Stream 2 and the Keystone XL pipeline, becomes a focal point of geopolitical contention, influencing regional dynamics and alliances.

- **Strategic Alliances:** Nations form strategic alliances based on energy considerations, with partnerships and conflicts influenced by the need for resource access and control.

- **Energy Security:** Ensuring a stable and secure energy supply is a cornerstone of energy diplomacy, influencing foreign policy decisions and military strategies.

4. Technological Advancements and Energy Diplomacy:

- **Renewable Energy Diplomacy:** The rise of renewable energy sources introduces new diplomatic considerations, as nations collaborate on clean energy initiatives and compete in the development and deployment of green technologies.

- **Technological Innovation:** Advancements in extraction technologies, such as hydraulic fracturing (fracking) and deep-sea drilling, reshape the energy landscape and impact diplomatic relations.

5. Environmental Implications:

- **Climate Change Diplomacy:** Climate change considerations become integral to energy diplomacy, influencing international agreements, emissions reduction targets, and the transition to sustainable energy sources.

- **Resource Extraction and Conservation:** Balancing the need for resource extraction with environmental conservation becomes a diplomatic challenge, as nations seek to exploit energy reserves while addressing ecological concerns.

6. Economic Considerations:

- **Energy Trade and Economic Power:** Energy exports contribute significantly to the economic power of exporting nations, shaping trade balances, revenue streams, and economic development.

- **Investment Diplomacy:** Nations engage in investment diplomacy to secure access to energy resources, with foreign direct investments, joint ventures, and infrastructure projects playing key roles.

7. Energy Diplomacy in Multilateral Forums:

- **Global Energy Governance:** Multilateral forums, including the United Nations Framework Convention on Climate Change (UNFCCC) and the G20, provide platforms for energy diplomacy, fostering cooperation, and shaping international energy policies.

- **Energy Summits and Organizations:** Specialized energy summits and organizations, like the World Energy Council, facilitate dialogue among nations, industry stakeholders, and experts, contributing to the development of global energy strategies.

8. Energy Transition and Diplomatic Challenges:

- **Shift to Renewables:** The global shift towards renewable energy sources poses diplomatic challenges as nations navigate the transition, addressing economic interests, geopolitical implications, and social considerations.

- **Dependency on Fossil Fuels:** Nations heavily dependent on fossil fuels face diplomatic pressures to diversify their energy mix, balancing economic interests with environmental responsibilities.

9. Challenges in Energy Diplomacy:

- **Resource Nationalism:** Resource-rich nations may adopt policies of resource nationalism, limiting foreign access to their energy reserves and challenging established international norms.

- **Geopolitical Conflicts:** Energy diplomacy is intertwined with geopolitical conflicts, as seen in disputes over the South China Sea, the Arctic, and the Eastern Mediterranean, where energy resources contribute to regional tensions.

- **Technological Disparities:** Disparities in technological capabilities and access to clean energy technologies create diplomatic challenges, especially in negotiations related to climate change mitigation.

10. Regional Dynamics and Case Studies:

- **Middle East:** The Middle East, with its abundant oil reserves, has long been a focal point of global energy diplomacy, shaping alliances, conflicts, and economic relationships.

- **Arctic Region:** The melting of Arctic ice opens new opportunities for resource extraction, leading to diplomatic contests over territory, resources, and shipping routes.

- **Africa:** African nations, with diverse energy resources, engage in diplomatic efforts to attract investments, ensure sustainable development, and address energy poverty.

11. Future Trends in Energy Diplomacy:

- **Hydrogen Diplomacy:** The development and export of green hydrogen emerge as a diplomatic focus, with nations positioning themselves as leaders in this nascent industry.

- **Space-based Energy:** Advances in space-based energy, including solar power harvested in space, introduce new diplomatic considerations as nations explore the potential for extraterrestrial resource utilization.

- **Digital Energy Diplomacy:** The integration of digital technologies, including smart grids, energy storage, and blockchain in the energy sector, reshapes diplomatic considerations and regulatory frameworks.

12. Ethical Considerations:

- **Environmental Justice:** Energy diplomacy raises ethical questions about environmental justice, as resource extraction may disproportionately impact marginalized communities and vulnerable ecosystems.

- **Access to Energy:** Ensuring universal access to energy becomes an ethical imperative, prompting diplomatic efforts to address energy poverty and inequality.

13. Public Perception and Advocacy:

- **Media Influence:** Media shapes public perception of energy diplomacy, influencing narratives on environmental sustainability, resource conflicts, and the role of nations in shaping global energy policies.

- **Civil Society Advocacy:** Civil society organizations play a role in energy diplomacy by advocating for sustainable practices, transparency, and social responsibility in energy projects.

14. Diplomatic Initiatives for Sustainable Energy:

- **Paris Agreement:** The Paris Agreement exemplifies a diplomatic initiative aimed at mitigating climate change by fostering international cooperation on emissions reduction and sustainable energy development.

- **International Solar Alliance:** Diplomatic efforts, such as the International Solar Alliance, focus on promoting solar energy adoption, particularly in regions with high solar potential.

15. Role of Energy in Geopolitical Influence:

- **Energy Superpowers:** Nations with significant energy resources, often referred to as energy superpowers, leverage their positions to exert geopolitical influence and shape global agendas.

- **Energy Independence:** Pursuit of energy independence influences diplomatic strategies, as nations seek to reduce dependency on external sources and enhance their geopolitical autonomy.

16. Education and Capacity Building:

- **Energy Diplomacy Education:** Educational initiatives in energy diplomacy are crucial for building the capacity of diplomats, policymakers, and energy professionals to navigate the complexities of the energy landscape.

- **Training in Renewable Technologies:** Capacity building in renewable energy technologies enhances diplomatic capabilities, fostering collaborations and knowledge-sharing among nations.

17. Conclusion: Energy Diplomacy, as a dynamic and multifaceted field, continues to be a critical factor in shaping the global geopolitical landscape. From historical struggles for control over fossil fuels to contemporary challenges posed by the energy transition, the interplay between energy and diplomacy underscores the intricate connections between national interests, environmental sustainability, and technological innovation. As nations navigate the complexities of the energy landscape, the imperative for diplomatic collaboration, ethical considerations, and global governance mechanisms becomes increasingly evident. Understanding the nuances of Energy Diplomacy is essential for fostering international cooperation, addressing climate challenges, and ensuring a sustainable and equitable energy future for the global community.

CHAPTER 33: CULTURAL DIPLOMACY: UNSPOKEN CONNECTIONS BETWEEN NATIONS

Cultural Diplomacy stands at the crossroads of international relations and the arts, forging unspoken connections between nations by leveraging the power of culture, heritage, and creativity. This in-depth exploration delves into the historical roots, key components, contemporary practices, and the profound impact of cultural diplomacy on shaping global perceptions, fostering mutual understanding, and building bridges in an interconnected world.

1. Historical Roots of Cultural Diplomacy:

- **Ancient Civilizations:** Cultural exchanges between ancient civilizations, such as the Silk Road connecting East and West, laid the groundwork for cross-cultural interactions and the exchange of ideas.

- **Renaissance and Cultural Diplomacy:** During the Renaissance, the Italian city-states used cultural diplomacy to enhance their prestige, with artists, scholars, and diplomats serving as ambassadors of culture.

- **Cold War Era:** The Cold War saw the use of cultural exchanges between the United States and the Soviet Union as a means to promote ideological values and reduce tensions.

2. Key Components of Cultural Diplomacy:

- **Arts and Entertainment:** Cultural diplomacy often

involves the promotion of arts, music, literature, theater, and film as vehicles for cross-cultural understanding and appreciation.

- **Language and Education:** Promoting language learning and educational exchanges fosters deeper cultural connections by facilitating direct communication and understanding.

- **Cultural Heritage:** Showcasing a nation's cultural heritage, including historical sites, museums, and traditions, serves as a powerful tool in cultural diplomacy.

- **Public Diplomacy:** Public engagement through cultural events, festivals, and exhibitions contributes to people-to-people connections, transcending political boundaries.

3. Contemporary Practices in Cultural Diplomacy:

- **International Festivals:** Cultural festivals, such as the Edinburgh Festival Fringe and the Cannes Film Festival, provide platforms for global cultural exchange and collaboration.

- **Artistic Residencies:** Cultural diplomacy often involves hosting artists and creators from one nation in another, fostering collaboration, and exposing diverse audiences to new perspectives.

- **Digital Platforms:** The use of digital platforms, including social media, online exhibitions, and virtual performances, extends the reach of cultural diplomacy, enabling global audiences to engage with diverse cultural expressions.

4. Soft Power and Cultural Diplomacy:

- **Soft Power Dynamics:** Cultural diplomacy is a

manifestation of soft power, where a nation's attractiveness, values, and cultural output influence international perceptions and relations.

- **Cultural Icons:** The global impact of cultural icons, from musicians to filmmakers, contributes to a nation's soft power, shaping positive narratives and fostering goodwill.

5. Bilateral Cultural Diplomacy Initiatives:

- **Goethe-Institut:** Germany's Goethe-Institut promotes German culture and language worldwide, fostering cultural exchange and cooperation.

- **British Council:** The British Council operates globally, organizing cultural programs and educational initiatives to strengthen ties between the UK and other nations.

- **Alliance Française:** France's Alliance Française network disseminates French language and culture, enhancing France's cultural influence globally.

6. Cultural Diplomacy in Conflict Resolution:

- **Cultural Understanding for Peace:** Cultural diplomacy plays a role in conflict resolution by promoting mutual understanding, tolerance, and respect for diverse perspectives.

- **Arts in Post-Conflict Zones:** Initiatives using art and culture in post-conflict zones, such as community-based theater and mural projects, contribute to healing and reconciliation.

7. Cultural Diplomacy and Tourism:

- **Cultural Tourism:** Cultural diplomacy and tourism are intertwined, as travelers experience and engage with the cultural richness of a destination, contributing to cross-cultural dialogue.

- **Heritage Preservation:** Preserving cultural heritage sites is not only a source of national pride but also a means to attract tourists and showcase a nation's history and traditions.

8. Challenges in Cultural Diplomacy:

- **Cultural Sensitivity:** Navigating cultural differences and avoiding misunderstandings requires cultural sensitivity in the planning and execution of diplomatic initiatives.

- **Political Instrumentalization:** Cultural diplomacy can face challenges when governments instrumentalize it for political purposes, potentially leading to misinterpretations and conflicts.

- **Access and Inclusivity:** Ensuring access to cultural diplomacy initiatives for diverse communities and avoiding elitism is crucial for fostering genuine cross-cultural connections.

9. Role of Cultural Diplomacy in Global Governance:

- **International Organizations:** Bodies like UNESCO (United Nations Educational, Scientific and Cultural Organization) play a role in promoting cultural diplomacy as a means to achieve global peace, understanding, and sustainable development.

- **Interconnected Global Challenges:** Cultural diplomacy is increasingly recognized as essential in addressing interconnected global challenges such as climate change, health crises, and migration.

10. Cultural Diplomacy and Global Events:

- **Olympic Games:** The Olympic Games serve as a global platform for cultural exchange, bringing together nations through sports, art, and cultural celebrations.

- **World Expositions:** Events like World Expos showcase a nation's cultural and technological achievements, promoting diplomatic ties and fostering collaboration.

11. Diaspora and Cultural Diplomacy:

- **Diaspora Contributions:** Diaspora communities contribute to cultural diplomacy by serving as cultural ambassadors, maintaining connections with their heritage, and fostering understanding between their host and home countries.

- **Cultural Hybridization:** Diaspora communities often embody cultural hybridization, influencing both their host culture and preserving aspects of their origin culture.

12. Educational Initiatives and Cultural Diplomacy:

- **Exchange Programs:** Student exchange programs, such as the Fulbright Program, foster cultural diplomacy by allowing individuals to immerse themselves in a foreign culture, promoting mutual understanding.

- **Cultural Education:** Integrating cultural education into school curricula enhances global awareness, promoting cultural diplomacy from an early age.

13. Technological Advancements and Cultural Diplomacy:

- **Virtual Cultural Exchanges:** Technology facilitates virtual cultural exchanges, allowing people to engage in cultural activities, attend events, and interact with cultural practitioners from anywhere in the world.

- **Digital Museums and Exhibitions:** Online platforms enable the creation of digital museums and exhibitions, expanding the reach of cultural diplomacy beyond physical boundaries.

14. Environmental and Sustainable Cultural Diplomacy:

- **Environmental Art:** Cultural diplomacy intersects

with environmental awareness through initiatives like environmental art exhibitions, highlighting the interconnectedness of culture and sustainability.

- **Cultural Practices for Sustainability:** Indigenous cultural practices that promote environmental stewardship contribute to a sustainable approach to cultural diplomacy.

15. Cultural Diplomacy and Gender Equality:

- **Empowering Women in the Arts:** Empowering women in cultural fields contributes to gender equality and enhances cultural diplomacy by amplifying diverse voices and perspectives.

- **Representation in Cultural Initiatives:** Ensuring representation and inclusion of women in cultural initiatives fosters an equitable and diverse cultural diplomacy landscape.

16. Public Diplomacy and Cultural Diplomacy:

- **Cultural Exchange Programs:** Public diplomacy initiatives, such as the Kennedy Center's Arts Ambassador Program, leverage cultural exchange to build people-to-people connections and promote diplomatic goals.

- **Cultural Diplomacy in Conflict Zones:** Public diplomacy interventions using culture, such as music and art festivals in conflict zones, aim to foster understanding and reconciliation among communities.

17. Ethical Considerations in Cultural Diplomacy:

- **Respect for Local Cultures:** Ethical cultural diplomacy requires a deep respect for local cultures, avoiding appropriation or imposition of cultural values.

- **Avoiding Stereotypes:** Cultural diplomacy initiatives must avoid perpetuating stereotypes, recognizing the diversity within cultures and avoiding a monolithic representation.

18. Future Trends in Cultural Diplomacy:

- **Digital Cultural Experiences:** The integration of augmented reality (AR) and virtual reality (VR) will enhance digital cultural experiences, allowing audiences to engage with cultural content in immersive ways.

- **Cultural Exchange Platforms:** Online platforms that facilitate direct connections between artists, creators, and audiences globally will continue to shape the landscape of cultural diplomacy.

- **Cultural Responses to Global Challenges:** Cultural diplomacy will increasingly play a role in addressing global challenges, with artistic expressions and cultural initiatives responding to issues like social justice, climate change, and pandemics.

19. Conclusion: Cultural diplomacy, as a dynamic force weaving unspoken connections between nations, transcends political, geographical, and linguistic boundaries. From historical exchanges to contemporary initiatives, the profound impact of cultural diplomacy lies in its ability to foster mutual respect, appreciation for diversity, and shared human experiences. As the world becomes more interconnected, the role of cultural diplomacy in shaping global narratives, influencing public perceptions, and building bridges of understanding becomes increasingly crucial. Nurturing these unspoken connections ensures that the rich tapestry of human cultures continues to contribute to the fabric of international relations, promoting a world where dialogue, creativity, and shared heritage lead the way to a more harmonious and interconnected future.

CHAPTER 34: SILENT ARBITERS: INTERNATIONAL ORGANIZATIONS AND GLOBAL GOVERNANCE

International organizations (IOs) have emerged as silent arbiters in the complex web of global governance, playing a pivotal role in shaping international relations, fostering cooperation, and addressing shared challenges. This comprehensive exploration delves into the historical evolution, functions, impact, challenges, and the evolving role of international organizations in the contemporary world, emphasizing their silent but influential role as arbiters of global affairs.

1. Historical Evolution of International Organizations:

- **League of Nations:** The League of Nations, established after World War I, was the first attempt at global governance. Although it faced challenges and ultimately failed, it laid the groundwork for future international cooperation.

- **United Nations:** The United Nations (UN), founded in 1945, is a central international organization aimed at promoting peace, security, and cooperation among nations. Its specialized agencies, such as UNESCO and WHO, contribute to various aspects of global governance.

2. Functions of International Organizations:

- **Peace and Security:** IOs like the UN Security Council address conflicts and promote peacekeeping missions, demonstrating their crucial role in maintaining global security.

- **Economic Cooperation:** Organizations like the International Monetary Fund (IMF) and the World Bank foster economic stability, development, and cooperation among member states.

- **Humanitarian Assistance:** IOs engage in humanitarian efforts, responding to crises, providing aid, and coordinating relief operations during natural disasters and conflicts.

- **Environmental Protection:** Global environmental challenges are addressed by organizations such as the United Nations Environment Programme (UNEP), which promotes sustainable practices and biodiversity conservation.

- **Human Rights Promotion:** IOs work to protect and promote human rights globally, with bodies like the United Nations Human Rights Council monitoring and addressing violations.

3. Impact of International Organizations on Global Governance:

- **Norm Setting:** IOs contribute to the development of international norms and standards, influencing state behavior and fostering a shared framework for global governance.

- **Conflict Resolution:** Through diplomatic efforts and peacekeeping missions, IOs play a critical role in mediating conflicts and preventing the escalation of hostilities.

- **Legal Frameworks:** International law is shaped by IOs, providing a legal framework for resolving disputes, ensuring accountability, and regulating issues like trade, human rights, and the environment.

4. The Evolving Landscape of Global Governance:

- **Multilateralism:** The rise of multilateralism reflects a shift towards collaborative governance, with IOs serving as platforms for nations to address common challenges and pursue shared goals.

- **Emerging Powers' Influence:** The influence of emerging powers in IOs, such as the BRICS countries, challenges traditional power dynamics and calls for a more inclusive global governance structure.

- **Civil Society Engagement:** IOs increasingly involve civil society organizations, promoting inclusivity and giving a voice to non-state actors in global decision-making processes.

5. Challenges Faced by International Organizations:

- **Power Imbalances:** Power imbalances among member states can hinder effective decision-making within IOs, with influential nations exerting disproportionate influence.

- **Resource Constraints:** IOs often face financial and resource constraints, limiting their capacity to address complex global challenges adequately.

- **Crisis Response Delays:** Bureaucratic processes within IOs may lead to delays in responding to crises, hampering their ability to provide timely assistance and intervention.

6. Specialized International Organizations:

- **World Health Organization (WHO):** The WHO plays a crucial role in global health governance, coordinating responses to pandemics, addressing public health issues, and setting international health standards.

- **International Labour Organization (ILO):** The ILO focuses on labor rights, social justice, and the promotion of decent work globally, contributing to the development of fair and equitable labor practices.

7. Regional Organizations and Global Governance:

- **European Union (EU):** The EU serves as a unique model of regional integration, influencing global governance through economic cooperation, security measures, and shared governance structures.

- **African Union (AU):** The AU addresses regional challenges in Africa, promoting peace, stability, and economic development through regional collaboration.

8. Technological Advances and Global Governance:

- **Digital Diplomacy:** The use of digital tools and platforms enhances the communication and coordination capabilities of IOs, enabling more efficient global governance.

- **Cybersecurity Challenges:** IOs grapple with emerging cybersecurity threats, requiring collaborative efforts to develop international norms and regulations.

9. Environmental Governance and International Organizations:

- **Paris Agreement:** The Paris Agreement, facilitated by the United Nations Framework Convention on Climate Change (UNFCCC), exemplifies global efforts to address climate change through cooperative governance and shared commitments.

- **Biodiversity Conservation:** IOs like the Convention on Biological Diversity (CBD) work to preserve global biodiversity through coordinated conservation efforts and the establishment of protected areas.

10. Role of International Organizations in Health Crises:

- **Pandemic Response:** IOs, particularly the WHO, play a central role in coordinating global responses to health crises, as seen in efforts to combat the COVID-19 pandemic through vaccine distribution, information dissemination, and resource mobilization.

- **Health Equity:** IOs work towards ensuring equitable access to healthcare resources, addressing disparities in health outcomes on a global scale.

11. Gender and International Organizations:

- **Women's Rights Advocacy:** IOs advocate for gender equality and women's rights, promoting initiatives that address discrimination, violence, and barriers to women's participation in various spheres of life.

- **UN Women:** The establishment of UN Women underscores the commitment of IOs to advancing gender equality globally, consolidating efforts to address gender-based challenges.

12. Cultural Diplomacy within International Organizations:

- **Promoting Cross-Cultural Understanding:** IOs foster cross-cultural understanding by promoting cultural exchange, dialogue, and initiatives that celebrate cultural diversity.

- **UNESCO's Cultural Programs:** UNESCO's initiatives focus on safeguarding cultural heritage, promoting cultural expressions, and fostering intercultural dialogue as tools for peace and mutual understanding.

13. Future Trends in Global Governance through International Organizations:

- **Digital Governance Platforms:** The integration of advanced technologies, including artificial intelligence and blockchain, may reshape governance structures within IOs, enhancing transparency and efficiency.

- **Global Health Governance Reform:** The experience of the COVID-19 pandemic may lead to reforms in global health governance, strengthening the capacity of IOs to respond to future health crises.

- **Enhanced Multilateralism:** The trend towards enhanced multilateralism may see IOs playing a more central role in addressing global challenges, with increased cooperation and coordination among member states.

14. Education and Capacity Building within International Organizations:

- **Training and Professional Development:** IOs invest in education and capacity-building programs to enhance the skills and knowledge of diplomats, policymakers, and professionals involved in global governance.

- **Partnerships with Academic Institutions:** Collaborations between IOs and academic institutions contribute to knowledge-sharing and research that informs global governance practices.

15. Ethical Considerations in International Organizations:

- **Human Rights Protections:** Upholding human rights is a cornerstone of ethical governance within IOs, requiring a commitment to protecting individuals from discrimination, violence, and oppression.

- **Transparency and Accountability:** Ensuring transparency and accountability in the decision-making processes of IOs is essential for maintaining public trust and legitimacy.

16. Public Perception and International Organizations:

- **Media Influence:** Media plays a significant role in shaping public perceptions of IOs, influencing narratives about their effectiveness, impact, and role in global affairs.

- **Civil Society Engagement:** Engaging with civil society organizations allows IOs to address public concerns, receive feedback, and enhance their responsiveness to global challenges.

17. Conclusion: International organizations, as silent arbiters of global governance, navigate the complexities of an interconnected world, addressing shared challenges and fostering collaboration among nations. From peace and security to economic cooperation, environmental sustainability, and public health, the multifaceted role of IOs underscores their significance in shaping the course of international relations. As the world continues to evolve, the adaptability, inclusivity, and ethical conduct of international organizations will be pivotal in ensuring effective and equitable global governance that meets the diverse needs of the international community. The silent but profound influence of these arbiters will continue to resonate in the pursuit of a more cooperative, just, and interconnected world.

CHAPTER 35: SILENT INNOVATIONS: TECHNOLOGY AS A DIPLOMATIC TOOL

In the ever-evolving landscape of international relations, the role of technology as a diplomatic tool has become increasingly pronounced. Silent Innovations refer to the transformative impact of technology on diplomatic practices, fostering communication, influencing geopolitical dynamics, and reshaping the traditional notions of statecraft. This extensive exploration delves into historical contexts, the multifaceted influence of technology, emerging trends, ethical considerations, and the broader implications of this silent but profound revolution in diplomatic affairs.

1. Historical Evolution of Technology in Diplomacy:

- **Telegraph and Diplomacy:** The telegraph, dating back to the 19th century, revolutionized diplomatic communication by enabling rapid transmission of messages across vast distances.

- **Radio and Broadcasting:** The advent of radio allowed for the dissemination of diplomatic messages to a global audience, influencing public opinion during significant geopolitical events.

- **Computers and Diplomatic Correspondence:** The integration of computers in diplomatic offices streamlined communication and data management, marking a significant leap in diplomatic efficiency.

2. Technology as a Catalyst for Global Connectivity:

- **Internet and Diplomacy:** The internet has

transformed diplomatic communication, facilitating instant and secure exchanges of information among diplomats, government officials, and international organizations.

- **Social Media Impact:** Platforms like Twitter and Facebook have become diplomatic tools, enabling leaders to communicate directly with global audiences, shaping narratives, and responding to geopolitical events in real-time.

3. Cyber Diplomacy and National Security:

- **Cybersecurity Challenges:** Technology's role in diplomacy extends to national security, with nations investing in cybersecurity measures to protect sensitive diplomatic communications from cyber threats.

- **Cyber Espionage:** The use of technology for espionage has become a silent but potent aspect of international relations, with nations employing sophisticated cyber tools to gather intelligence.

4. Digital Diplomacy and Public Engagement:

- **E-Diplomacy Initiatives:** Governments utilize digital platforms for e-diplomacy initiatives, engaging with the public, fostering citizen diplomacy, and providing real-time updates on diplomatic activities.

- **Virtual Diplomatic Summits:** The COVID-19 pandemic accelerated the adoption of virtual summits, showcasing how technology can enable global leaders to convene and address critical issues remotely.

5. Technological Diplomacy in Conflict Resolution:

- **Conflict Mapping and Analysis:** Technology aids diplomats in analyzing and understanding conflicts by utilizing data analytics, satellite imagery, and mapping tools to assess complex geopolitical situations.

- **Digital Peacekeeping:** Technology supports peacekeeping efforts by enhancing surveillance, communication, and coordination in conflict zones, contributing to more effective conflict resolution.

6. Artificial Intelligence (AI) and Diplomatic Strategy:

- **Predictive Analytics:** AI is employed in diplomatic circles for predictive analytics, helping anticipate geopolitical developments, assess potential risks, and formulate proactive strategies.

- **Language Translation Tools:** AI-driven language translation tools facilitate communication between diplomats who speak different languages, breaking down linguistic barriers.

7. Blockchain Technology in Diplomacy:

- **Secure Diplomatic Communications:** Blockchain ensures secure and tamper-proof communication, enhancing the confidentiality and integrity of diplomatic exchanges.

- **Digital Diplomatic Agreements:** Blockchain technology is explored for creating smart contracts and digital agreements, providing a transparent and verifiable framework for diplomatic commitments.

8. Space Technology and Global Surveillance:

- **Satellite Diplomacy:** Space technology contributes to global surveillance and reconnaissance, offering diplomats valuable insights into military activities, environmental changes, and disaster response.

- **Space Diplomacy:** The exploration and utilization

of outer space raise diplomatic considerations, with nations collaborating on space missions, satellite launches, and space research.

9. Quantum Diplomacy:

- **Quantum Encryption:** Quantum technology introduces new possibilities for secure communication through quantum encryption, safeguarding diplomatic messages from potential breaches.

- **Quantum Computing and Diplomatic Simulation:** Quantum computing holds promise for enhancing diplomatic simulations, allowing for more complex and accurate modeling of international relations scenarios.

10. Ethical Considerations in Technological Diplomacy:

- **Privacy Concerns:** The use of technology in diplomacy raises concerns about privacy, especially when surveillance tools and data analytics are employed without adequate safeguards.

- **Weaponization of Technology:** Nations must navigate the ethical implications of potentially weaponizing technology for diplomatic purposes, balancing innovation with responsible use.

11. Technological Diplomacy in Economic Relations:

- **Digital Trade Agreements:** Technology facilitates the negotiation and implementation of digital trade agreements, addressing issues related to e-commerce, data flow, and intellectual property.

- **Cryptocurrencies and Economic Diplomacy:**

Cryptocurrencies and blockchain technologies impact economic diplomacy by introducing new forms of digital currency and financial transactions.

12. Environmental Diplomacy and Technology:

- **Climate Modeling:** Technology aids in climate modeling and data analysis, supporting diplomatic efforts to address environmental challenges and formulate international agreements.

- **Renewable Energy Diplomacy:** The development and sharing of renewable energy technologies through diplomatic channels contribute to global efforts to combat climate change.

13. Technological Diplomacy and Global Health:

- **Telemedicine Diplomacy:** The use of telemedicine technologies supports diplomatic initiatives in global health, enabling remote consultations, information exchange, and collaborative research.

- **Vaccine Diplomacy:** Technology plays a crucial role in the distribution and administration of vaccines, contributing to diplomatic initiatives aimed at addressing global health crises.

14. International Collaboration in Scientific and Technological Innovation:

- **Research Collaborations:** Diplomacy fosters international collaboration in scientific research and technological innovation, promoting the sharing of knowledge and advancements for the benefit of humanity.

- **Joint Technological Projects:** Collaborative projects, such as the International Space Station (ISS), exemplify how nations can work together on complex technological endeavors, transcending geopolitical differences.

15. Future Trends in Technological Diplomacy:

- **5G Technology and Diplomacy:** The widespread adoption of 5G technology will enhance connectivity and communication, influencing diplomatic practices and enabling new forms of digital interaction.

- **Emergence of New Technologies:** Technologies like quantum computing, biotechnology, and neurotechnology will likely introduce novel dimensions to diplomatic strategy and engagement.

- **Artificial Intelligence in Decision-Making:** The integration of AI into diplomatic decision-making processes may become more prevalent, offering insights and recommendations based on vast data sets.

16. Diplomatic Education and Capacity Building:

- **Technology in Diplomatic Training:** Diplomatic academies and training programs incorporate technology to educate diplomats on the latest tools, platforms, and strategies for effective diplomatic engagement.

- **E-Learning Platforms:** Online platforms offer diplomats opportunities for continuous learning, enabling them to stay updated on technological advancements and their implications for diplomacy.

17. Technological Diplomacy and Cultural Exchange:

- **Virtual Cultural Diplomacy:** Technology facilitates virtual cultural exchanges, allowing nations to showcase their cultural heritage, artistic expressions, and innovations on a global stage.

- **Digital Cultural Collaboration:** Cross-border collaborations in the arts, literature, and creative industries leverage technology to bridge cultural gaps and foster mutual understanding.

18. Public Perception and Technological Diplomacy:

- **Media Influence:** Media plays a critical role in shaping public perceptions of technological diplomacy, influencing narratives about the benefits, risks, and ethical considerations associated with the use of technology in international relations.

- **Social Media and Diplomatic Narratives:** The use of social media platforms by diplomats and leaders shapes diplomatic narratives, influencing how global audiences perceive diplomatic initiatives and technological advancements.

19. Conclusion: Silent Innovations mark a paradigm shift in the way nations engage with one another on the global stage. Technology, as a diplomatic tool, transcends borders, fosters connectivity, and introduces unprecedented opportunities and challenges. From cybersecurity to space exploration, from AI-driven diplomacy to digital trade agreements, the silent innovations shaping diplomatic practices are vast and diverse. Navigating the ethical considerations, harnessing the potential for collaboration, and staying abreast of emerging trends will be imperative for nations as they leverage technology as a silent yet potent force in the intricate dance of international relations. The silent innovations of today are the foundation upon which the diplomacy of tomorrow will be built, reshaping the world in ways that are both profound and, at times, imperceptible.

CHAPTER 36: THE SILENT FRONTIER: OUTER SPACE AND THE NEW GEOPOLITICAL REALM

The vast expanse of outer space, once the exclusive domain of scientific exploration and cosmic curiosity, has evolved into the new geopolitical frontier, silently shaping the future of global politics. The Silent Frontier encompasses the strategic, economic, and technological dimensions of space exploration, raising profound questions about sovereignty, international cooperation, and the balance of power. This comprehensive exploration delves into the historical context, current dynamics, emerging challenges, and the transformative potential of outer space in the geopolitical landscape.

1. Historical Context of Space Exploration:

- **Space Race and Cold War:** The rivalry between the United States and the Soviet Union during the Cold War era spurred the Space Race, marking the first steps of human exploration beyond Earth. The geopolitical significance of achieving space milestones heightened global competition.

2. The Geopolitical Significance of Space:

- **Strategic Importance:** Satellites play a crucial role in communication, navigation, weather monitoring, and intelligence gathering, making control over space assets strategically vital for military and economic reasons.

- **Global Connectivity:** Space-based technologies facilitate global connectivity, influencing economic and diplomatic relations by enabling instant communication, financial transactions, and information sharing.

3. Commercialization of Space:

- **Private Space Companies:** The rise of private space companies, exemplified by SpaceX and Blue Origin, introduces new actors in space exploration, challenging traditional state dominance and altering the geopolitical landscape.

- **Resource Extraction:** The potential for resource extraction, including rare minerals and water, raises questions about ownership, international agreements, and the economic implications of space commerce.

4. The Role of International Space Treaties:

- **Outer Space Treaty:** The Outer Space Treaty, established in 1967, lays the foundation for international space law. It promotes the peaceful use of outer space, prohibits the placement of weapons, and emphasizes cooperation in exploration.

- **Moon Agreement and Controversies:** The Moon Agreement, although signed by several nations, has not been ratified by major space-faring countries, leading to debates about the legal framework for lunar resource utilization.

5. Military Dimensions of Space:

- **Space Militarization:** The militarization of space involves the development and deployment of military assets in orbit, raising concerns about the weaponization of outer space and the potential for conflict escalation.

- **Anti-Satellite (ASAT) Weapons:** ASAT capabilities pose a threat to space assets, contributing to a new form of geopolitical competition and heightening tensions among space-faring nations.

6. International Space Station (ISS) and Diplomacy:

- **Symbol of Cooperation:** The ISS stands as a symbol of international cooperation, involving space agencies from the United States, Russia, Europe, Japan, and Canada. It showcases the potential for peaceful collaboration despite geopolitical differences.

- **Future of ISS and Commercialization:** Discussions about the future of the ISS, potential commercialization, and the involvement of private entities add new layers to diplomatic considerations in space exploration.

7. Emerging Players in Space Exploration:

- **China's Ambitions:** China has rapidly developed its space capabilities, with lunar exploration missions, plans for a space station, and ambitions for crewed Mars missions. Its rise as a space power introduces geopolitical complexities.

- **India's Space Program:** India's space program, highlighted by its Mars Orbiter Mission, signifies the increasing role of emerging nations in space exploration, influencing regional and global diplomatic dynamics.

8. Space and Economic Competitiveness:

- **Satellite Industry:** The satellite industry, driven by communication, Earth observation, and navigation services, contributes significantly to national economies. The control and utilization of satellite networks become crucial for economic competitiveness.

- **Global Navigation Systems:** Nations invest in global navigation systems like GPS, GLONASS, and Galileo for military, economic, and diplomatic reasons, underlining the geopolitical importance of space-based navigation.

9. Space Tourism and Soft Power:

- **Emergence of Space Tourism:** The advent of space tourism, with companies like Virgin Galactic and Blue Origin offering suborbital flights, introduces a new dimension of soft power and diplomatic influence for nations investing in this industry.

- **Cultural Impact:** Nations engaging in space tourism showcase technological prowess, fostering national pride and influencing global perceptions, contributing to soft power diplomacy.

10. Space Exploration and Environmental Diplomacy:

- **Earth Observation for Climate Monitoring:** Satellites contribute to environmental diplomacy by providing crucial data for climate monitoring, disaster response, and environmental conservation, highlighting the interconnectedness of space and Earth diplomacy.

- **Space Debris Mitigation:** Diplomatic efforts are underway to address the issue of space debris, with collaborative initiatives to prevent further debris creation and ensure the sustainability of outer space activities.

11. Technological Innovation in Space Diplomacy:

- **Advancements in Propulsion Systems:** Innovations in propulsion systems, including ion drives and nuclear propulsion, influence the feasibility of deep space exploration and shape diplomatic considerations for interplanetary missions.

- **Space-Based Renewable Energy:** The exploration of space-based solar power as a renewable energy source introduces diplomatic considerations related to energy security and resource allocation.

12. Ethical Considerations in Outer Space:

- **Space Sustainability:** Diplomacy plays a role in addressing ethical concerns related to space sustainability, including responsible space debris management, orbital congestion, and the long-term impact of human activities on celestial bodies.

- **Planetary Protection:** The ethical imperative of planetary protection, preventing contamination of celestial bodies with Earth organisms during exploration, raises diplomatic questions about responsible space exploration.

13. The Lunar and Martian Frontiers:

- **Return to the Moon:** Lunar exploration has reemerged as a geopolitical objective, with plans for crewed missions and the establishment of lunar bases, leading to discussions about territorial rights and international collaboration.

- **Mars Colonization:** Ambitions for Mars colonization introduce diplomatic challenges related to resource allocation, international cooperation, and the potential establishment of extraterrestrial settlements.

14. Public-Private Partnerships and Diplomacy:

- **Collaboration with Private Entities:** Diplomacy extends to public-private partnerships, with governments collaborating with private companies in space exploration, raising questions about regulatory frameworks, liability, and shared objectives.

- **Global Impact:** The global impact of private entities in space, both economically and technologically, introduces a new dimension to diplomatic engagements, requiring adaptable frameworks and international cooperation.

15. Cultural Diplomacy and Space Exploration:

- **Global Space Events:** Events such as moon landings, Mars rover missions, and space exploration milestones become opportunities for cultural diplomacy, fostering a sense of shared humanity and inspiring international collaboration.

- **Representation and Diversity:** Diplomatic considerations extend to the representation of diverse cultures and nations in space exploration initiatives, shaping narratives that resonate globally.

16. Future Trends in Geopolitics of Outer Space:

- **Colonization and Governance:** As aspirations for space colonization evolve, discussions about governance, legal frameworks, and the role of international institutions in overseeing extraterrestrial activities will become central to future diplomatic efforts.

- **Interstellar Exploration:** The potential for interstellar exploration introduces speculative yet intriguing diplomatic considerations about humanity's role in the broader cosmos, transcending the confines of Earth-based geopolitics.

17. Education and Capacity Building in Space Diplomacy:

- **International Space Education Programs:** Diplomacy extends to educational initiatives that promote international collaboration in space science and technology, fostering a new generation of diplomats and scientists with a global perspective.

- **Capacity Building for Emerging Space Nations:** Collaborative efforts to build space capabilities in emerging nations contribute to diplomatic outreach, promoting inclusivity and ensuring the peaceful use of outer space.

18. Public Perception and Outer Space Diplomacy:

- **Media Narratives:** The narratives crafted by media influence public perceptions of outer space activities and diplomacy, shaping attitudes toward national space programs and international collaborations.

- **Engagement with Civil Society:** Diplomatic efforts in outer space activities increasingly involve engagement with civil society, as public interest and awareness contribute to the legitimacy and success of space missions.

19. Conclusion: The Silent Frontier, once the cosmic realm of scientific discovery, has transformed into a geopolitical arena with implications that extend far beyond the boundaries of Earth. As nations and private entities venture into the vastness of outer space, diplomacy takes on a new set of challenges and opportunities. From the militarization of space to the commercialization of cosmic resources, the geopolitics of outer space are multifaceted, requiring international collaboration, ethical considerations, and innovative governance frameworks. As humanity continues its exploration of the cosmos, the diplomatic frontier expands, necessitating adaptability, cooperation, and a shared commitment to the responsible and sustainable use of the Silent Frontier for the benefit of all. Outer space, once the silent void, now resonates with the echoes of geopolitical ambitions and diplomatic endeavors that will shape the future of humanity's cosmic journey.

CHAPTER 37: MARITIME DIPLOMACY: NAVIGATING TROUBLED WATERS

Maritime diplomacy, the art and practice of managing international relations through the lens of maritime interests, is a multifaceted endeavor that involves the strategic use of naval power, negotiation of maritime boundaries, protection of sea lanes, and cooperation on global maritime issues. Navigating troubled waters, both literally and metaphorically, encompasses the challenges and opportunities that nations face in the maritime domain. This extensive exploration delves into the historical context, contemporary dynamics, key elements of maritime diplomacy, and the geopolitical significance of managing maritime challenges amid a complex international landscape.

1. Historical Context of Maritime Diplomacy:

- **Age of Exploration:** Maritime diplomacy has roots in the Age of Exploration when seafaring nations engaged in diplomatic relations to establish trade routes and expand colonial empires.

- **Naval Power and Imperial Expansion:** The rise of naval power, exemplified by the British Royal Navy, played a pivotal role in shaping diplomatic relations and global power dynamics during the era of imperial expansion.

2. Strategic Elements of Maritime Diplomacy:

- **Naval Power Projection:** Maritime nations employ naval forces not only for national defense but also as instruments of power projection, influencing diplomatic negotiations and deterring potential adversaries.

- **Geopolitical Significance of Sea Control:** Controlling key maritime routes, such as chokepoints and straits, holds immense geopolitical significance, impacting global trade, energy security, and military access.

3. Maritime Boundaries and Territorial Disputes:

- **Exclusive Economic Zones (EEZs):** Negotiating and defining EEZs are crucial aspects of maritime diplomacy, with nations seeking to secure their economic interests and access to marine resources.

- **Territorial Disputes:** Contentious maritime territorial disputes, such as those in the South China Sea, challenge diplomatic relations, requiring careful negotiation to prevent escalation and find mutually acceptable solutions.

4. Piracy and Maritime Security:

- **Counter-Piracy Operations:** Maritime diplomacy addresses the challenge of piracy through international cooperation, joint naval patrols, and agreements to secure vital sea lanes, particularly in regions like the Gulf of Aden.

- **Transnational Maritime Crimes:** Diplomatic efforts extend to combatting transnational crimes at sea, including drug trafficking, human smuggling, and illegal fishing, necessitating collaborative frameworks.

5. Protection of Sea Lanes and Global Trade:

- **Strategic Importance of Sea Lanes:** Sea lanes, vital conduits for global trade, require diplomatic attention to ensure their security and prevent disruptions that could have far-reaching economic consequences.

- **International Maritime Conventions:** Diplomatic negotiations result in the establishment of international conventions, such as the United Nations Convention on the Law of the Sea (UNCLOS), which govern the rights and responsibilities of nations in maritime zones.

6. Environmental Diplomacy and Maritime Sustainability:

- **Marine Environmental Protection:** Diplomacy plays a role in addressing maritime environmental challenges, including oil spills, plastic pollution, and overfishing, through international agreements and collaborative initiatives.

- **Climate Change and Sea-Level Rise:** The impact of climate change on maritime regions requires diplomatic cooperation to mitigate environmental threats and adapt to changes, particularly in vulnerable coastal areas.

7. Arctic Diplomacy and the Melting Ice:

- **Arctic Governance:** The melting of Arctic ice opens new maritime routes and access to resources, sparking diplomatic efforts to establish governance structures, delineate boundaries, and address environmental concerns in the region.

- **Competition for Resources:** Arctic nations engage in diplomatic negotiations to manage the competition for oil, gas, and mineral resources, balancing economic interests with environmental preservation.

8. Role of Naval Diplomacy:

- **Naval Cooperation and Exercises:** Naval diplomacy involves joint exercises, port visits, and cooperation between navies to build trust, enhance interoperability, and contribute to regional stability.

- **Humanitarian Assistance and Disaster Relief (HADR):** Naval forces engage in diplomatic endeavors through HADR missions, responding to natural disasters and crises to provide assistance and build goodwill.

9. Geoeconomics and Maritime Silk Road:

- **Belt and Road Initiative (BRI):** China's BRI includes the Maritime Silk Road, a geoeconomic initiative that fosters maritime connectivity, infrastructure development, and economic partnerships, influencing maritime diplomacy in the Indo-Pacific region.

- **Economic Statecraft:** Nations employ economic statecraft in maritime diplomacy, leveraging economic incentives, infrastructure projects, and trade agreements to secure strategic interests and build geopolitical influence.

10. Soft Power and Cultural Diplomacy:

- **Naval Soft Power:** Naval capabilities, including hospital ships, cultural exchanges through naval visits, and participation in international maritime events, contribute to a nation's soft power and positive diplomatic image.

- **Cultural Diplomacy through Maritime Heritage:** Celebrating maritime heritage, historical maritime connections, and shared maritime traditions enhances cultural diplomacy and fosters mutual understanding among maritime nations.

11. International Organizations and Maritime Governance:

- **International Maritime Organization (IMO):** The IMO, a specialized agency of the United Nations, facilitates diplomatic cooperation to establish regulations, standards, and conventions governing maritime safety, security, and environmental protection.

- **Regional Maritime Organizations:** Regional bodies, such as the European Maritime Safety Agency (EMSA) and the Indian Ocean Rim Association (IORA), contribute to regional maritime diplomacy, addressing shared challenges and fostering cooperation.

12. Blue Economy and Sustainable Development:

- **Maritime Economic Development:** Diplomatic efforts focus on harnessing the blue economy, including sustainable fisheries, aquaculture, renewable energy from the ocean, and responsible tourism, to promote economic development and address maritime challenges.

- **International Collaboration for Ocean Exploration:** Diplomacy facilitates international collaboration in ocean exploration, scientific research, and the preservation of marine biodiversity through initiatives like the High Seas Alliance.

13. The Role of Technology in Maritime Diplomacy:

- **Maritime Domain Awareness (MDA):** Technology, including satellite surveillance, radar systems, and information-sharing platforms, enhances MDA, allowing nations to monitor maritime activities and respond to potential threats.

- **Unmanned Maritime Systems:** The use of unmanned underwater vehicles (UUVs) and unmanned aerial vehicles (UAVs) contributes to maritime diplomacy by providing cost-effective solutions for surveillance and reconnaissance.

14. Human Security and Maritime Diplomacy:

- **Combatting Illegal Migration:** Diplomacy addresses the challenges of illegal migration by fostering cooperation among nations to address root causes, enhance border control, and protect the human security of migrants at sea.

- **Maritime Search and Rescue Coordination:** Cooperation in maritime search and rescue operations exemplifies the diplomatic imperative to ensure the safety and well-being of individuals in distress at sea.

15. Naval Arms Control and Disarmament:

- **Arms Control Agreements:** Diplomacy extends to arms control agreements related to naval forces, aiming to prevent arms races, reduce tensions, and promote stability in maritime regions.

- **Non-Proliferation Efforts:** Diplomatic initiatives address concerns related to the proliferation of naval nuclear capabilities, promoting non-proliferation agreements and transparency measures.

16. Legal Disputes and Arbitration:

- **UNCLOS Dispute Resolution Mechanisms:** Nations engage in maritime diplomacy through UNCLOS dispute resolution mechanisms, such as the International Tribunal for the Law of the Sea (ITLOS) and arbitral tribunals, to address legal disputes related to maritime boundaries.

- **Bilateral and Multilateral Agreements:** Diplomatic negotiations lead to bilateral and multilateral agreements that provide frameworks for resolving legal disputes and managing shared maritime spaces.

17. Challenges to Maritime Diplomacy:

- **Great Power Competition:** The resurgence of great power competition, particularly among major maritime nations, poses challenges to maritime diplomacy, requiring careful navigation to prevent conflicts and foster cooperation.

- **Non-State Actors:** Diplomacy must contend with non-state actors, including pirate groups, transnational criminal organizations, and private maritime security firms, whose activities can disrupt maritime stability.

18. Future Trends in Maritime Diplomacy:

- **Emerging Maritime Technologies:** The integration of

emerging technologies, such as artificial intelligence, quantum computing, and autonomous vessels, will influence the future landscape of maritime diplomacy, requiring nations to adapt their strategies and policies.

- **Climate-Induced Challenges:** Rising sea levels, changing ocean currents, and extreme weather events will pose new challenges to maritime diplomacy, necessitating international cooperation to address climate-induced impacts on maritime security.

19. Conclusion: Maritime diplomacy, a dynamic and indispensable component of international relations, involves the careful navigation of complex and often troubled waters. From historical rivalries to contemporary challenges, nations engage in maritime diplomacy to secure their interests, foster cooperation, and address shared concerns on the high seas. The interplay of naval power, economic interests, environmental sustainability, and technological advancements underscores the multifaceted nature of maritime diplomacy. As nations confront the intricate geopolitical currents of the maritime domain, the ability to navigate troubled waters with diplomacy, cooperation, and strategic foresight becomes paramount. The future of maritime diplomacy will be shaped by emerging challenges, evolving technologies, and the collective commitment of nations to uphold the principles of the law of the sea, ensuring a stable and cooperative maritime order for the benefit of all.

CHAPTER 38: SILENT PARTNERSHIPS: UNLIKELY ALLIANCES IN GLOBAL POLITICS

Global politics is a complex tapestry woven with alliances and rivalries, often governed by shared interests and strategic objectives. Within this intricate landscape, the concept of silent partnerships emerges—a phenomenon where nations form alliances that might not align with conventional expectations. These unlikely collaborations, often strategic and discreet, are driven by geopolitical realities, economic imperatives, or shared concerns. This comprehensive exploration delves into the historical precedents, contemporary examples, and the nuanced dynamics that define silent partnerships, unraveling the intricacies of these unconventional alliances in the ever-evolving realm of global politics.

1. Historical Perspectives on Unlikely Alliances:

- **World War II Alliances:** The grand alliances of World War II, such as the alliance between the United States, the Soviet Union, and the United Kingdom, exemplify historical instances where nations with differing ideologies formed strategic partnerships to confront a common adversary.

- **Balance of Power Diplomacy:** Throughout history, states have engaged in balance of power diplomacy, forming alliances that might appear counterintuitive at first glance but serve to maintain stability and prevent the dominance of a single power.

2. Geoeconomic Silent Partnerships:

- **Economic Cooperation Amid Political Differences:**

Nations often engage in silent partnerships for economic reasons, setting aside political differences to foster trade and mutual economic benefits. Examples include China's economic ties with countries in Southeast Asia despite geopolitical tensions.

- **Energy Partnerships:** Geoeconomic considerations often drive silent partnerships in the energy sector, where nations collaborate for resource access, infrastructure development, and energy security.

3. Security and Counterterrorism Alliances:

- **Counterterrorism Cooperation:** Nations facing common threats from terrorism may form silent partnerships to share intelligence, coordinate security measures, and address the transnational nature of modern security challenges.

- **Military Cooperation in Regional Conflicts:** Silent military partnerships may emerge in regional conflicts where nations with divergent political ideologies join forces to counter a perceived common threat.

4. Environmental and Climate Change Alliances:

- **Climate Change Agreements:** Despite political differences, nations may enter into silent partnerships to address climate change, recognizing the shared responsibility for environmental sustainability and the need for collective action.

- **Natural Resource Management:** Silent collaborations on environmental issues, such as water resource management or biodiversity conservation, showcase instances where nations prioritize shared ecological concerns over political disparities.

5. Health Diplomacy and Global Pandemics:

- **Collaboration During Global Health Crises:** The outbreak of global pandemics, like the COVID-19 pandemic, may lead to silent partnerships as nations work together to combat the common threat, sharing medical expertise, vaccines, and resources.

- **International Health Organizations:** Silent partnerships often manifest through collaboration with international health organizations, highlighting the recognition of the interconnectedness of global health.

6. Regional Alliances and Unlikely Cohorts:

- **Regional Stability Considerations:** Nations in a specific region may form silent partnerships to maintain stability, counterbalance regional powers, or address common regional challenges.

- **Economic Integration:** Economic blocs and regional organizations often witness silent partnerships among member states, fostering economic integration and regional development.

7. Technology and Innovation Alliances:

- **Cross-Border Research and Innovation:** In the realm of technology and innovation, silent partnerships emerge as nations collaborate on research and development projects, leveraging complementary strengths to advance technological frontiers.

- **Intellectual Property Sharing:** Despite competitive aspects, silent partnerships may involve the sharing of intellectual property or collaborative efforts in technological domains where joint innovation benefits all parties.

8. Cultural and Educational Collaborations:

- **Soft Power Dynamics:** Silent partnerships in cultural and educational exchanges contribute to soft power dynamics, fostering understanding and goodwill between nations with diverse cultural backgrounds.

- **People-to-People Diplomacy:** Collaborations in academia, arts, and cultural initiatives serve as channels for people-to-people diplomacy, promoting dialogue and mutual appreciation despite political differences.

9. Crisis Diplomacy and Conflict Resolution:

- **Mediation in Regional Conflicts:** Nations may engage in silent partnerships to mediate in regional conflicts, offering diplomatic solutions and playing a role in conflict resolution, even when they have no direct stake in the dispute.

- **Humanitarian Interventions:** Silent partnerships can form during humanitarian crises, with nations contributing resources, expertise, and aid to address the immediate needs of affected populations.

10. Non-State Actors and Unofficial Alliances:

- **NGOs and Civil Society Collaborations:** Non-state actors, including non-governmental organizations (NGOs), may form silent partnerships with nations to address shared goals in areas such as human rights, environmental conservation, and social justice.

- **Corporate Alliances:** Economic interests often drive silent partnerships between nations and multinational corporations, where states collaborate with businesses to achieve shared economic objectives.

11. Soft Balancing and Hedging Strategies:

- **Soft Balancing Against Power Hegemony:** Silent partnerships may emerge as a form of soft balancing, where nations collaborate to counterbalance the influence of a dominant global power without engaging in overt confrontation.

- **Hedging Strategies in Uncertain Geopolitical Environments:** Nations may adopt hedging strategies, forming silent partnerships to diversify their diplomatic options and navigate uncertain geopolitical landscapes.

12. Diplomacy in Multilateral Forums:

- **UN and Multilateral Diplomacy:** Silent partnerships often play out in multilateral forums like the United Nations, where nations align on specific issues, vote together, or collaborate behind the scenes to influence global governance structures.

- **Coalitions of the Willing:** Informal coalitions of nations, formed for specific objectives, exemplify the flexibility and adaptability of silent partnerships in addressing pressing global challenges.

13. Economic Sanctions and Covert Alliances:

- **Covert Economic Alliances:** In response to economic sanctions or geopolitical isolation, nations may form covert economic alliances, engaging in trade or financial partnerships that are discreet to avoid international scrutiny.

- **Sanctions Evasion:** Silent partnerships may emerge as a means to evade international sanctions, with nations finding alternative routes for trade or financial transactions through collaborative efforts.

14. Intelligence Sharing and Cybersecurity Collaborations:

- **Counterterrorism Intelligence:** Silent partnerships in intelligence sharing are crucial in the fight against global terrorism, allowing nations to pool resources and expertise to counter common threats.

- **Cybersecurity Cooperation:** Nations facing cyber threats may form silent partnerships in cybersecurity, sharing information and collaborating on defensive strategies to mitigate the impact of cyber-attacks.

15. The Role of Global Institutions and Think Tanks:

- **Think Tank Networks:** Global think tanks and research institutions contribute to silent partnerships by fostering dialogue, generating policy recommendations, and providing platforms for informal diplomatic engagement.

- **International Organizations as Facilitators:** International organizations often facilitate silent partnerships by providing neutral ground for diplomatic interactions and collaborative initiatives.

16. Unspoken Agendas and the Limitations of Silent Partnerships:

- **Unspoken Agendas:** Silent partnerships may involve unspoken agendas and hidden motivations, raising questions about transparency, trust, and the potential for divergent interests.

- **Limitations of Secrecy:** While discretion is a hallmark of silent partnerships, the limitations of secrecy include the potential for misunderstandings, lack of accountability, and the risk of destabilizing the international order.

17. Contemporary Examples of Silent Partnerships:

- **Russia and Turkey:** Despite historical tensions, Russia and Turkey have formed silent partnerships in areas such as energy cooperation, regional diplomacy, and joint efforts in conflict zones.

- **Israel and Gulf States:** Recent diplomatic normalization between Israel and Gulf states, driven by shared concerns about regional stability and economic interests, represents a contemporary example of silent partnerships.

18. Global Power Shifts and Evolving Silent Alliances:

- **Rise of Multipolarity:** The evolving global order, characterized by the rise of multipolarity, is reshaping traditional alliances and fostering the emergence of new silent partnerships among nations with shared interests.

- **Shifting Alliances in Asia-Pacific:** The Asia-Pacific region, with its dynamic geopolitical landscape, witnesses shifting alliances and silent partnerships as nations adapt to changing power dynamics.

19. The Future of Silent Partnerships in Global Politics:

- **Adaptability in a Dynamic World:** The future of silent partnerships lies in nations' ability to adapt to a dynamic world, recognizing the impermanence of traditional alliances and the need for flexible diplomatic strategies.

- **Ethical Considerations and Global Governance:** As silent partnerships become more prevalent, ethical considerations and the role of global governance mechanisms will play a crucial role in shaping the norms and boundaries of these unconventional alliances.

Conclusion: Silent partnerships, as a nuanced aspect of global politics, weave a complex web of relationships that transcend conventional alliances. Whether driven by economic interests, shared security concerns, or a convergence of diplomatic objectives, these unlikely collaborations shape the course of international relations. Navigating the terrain of silent partnerships requires a delicate balance of strategic acumen, adaptability, and an understanding of the ever-evolving geopolitical landscape. As the world continues to grapple with multifaceted challenges, the role of silent partnerships in global politics is poised to grow, influencing diplomatic strategies and redefining the traditional paradigms of international alliances. Understanding the dynamics and implications of silent partnerships is essential for policymakers, diplomats, and scholars seeking insights into the intricate dance of nations on the global stage.

CHAPTER 39: THE SILENT REVOLUTIONARIES: MOVEMENTS SHAPING POLITICAL LANDSCAPES

The phrase "Silent Revolutionaries" encapsulates a diverse array of movements that, while not always grabbing the headlines, play a transformative role in shaping political landscapes across the globe. These movements, often rooted in societal shifts, technological advancements, or changing cultural norms, bring about gradual and profound changes in political structures, ideologies, and governance paradigms. This in-depth exploration delves into historical antecedents, contemporary examples, and the overarching impact of these silent revolutionaries, unveiling the intricate ways in which they influence the course of political evolution.

1. Historical Context of Silent Revolutionaries:

- **The Enlightenment:** The Enlightenment era, marked by intellectual and cultural changes in the 17th and 18th centuries, laid the foundation for silent revolutionaries by promoting ideas of individual liberty, reason, and the questioning of traditional authority.

- **Industrial Revolution:** The Industrial Revolution, with its socio-economic transformations, acted as a silent revolutionary force, giving rise to new social classes, urbanization, and the seeds of modern political ideologies.

2. Technological Revolution and Information Age:

- **The Digital Transformation:** The advent of the Information Age and the rise of the internet represent a silent revolutionary force, empowering individuals with access to information, fostering connectivity, and challenging traditional structures of communication.

- **Social Media Movements:** Platforms like Twitter, Facebook, and Instagram have become catalysts for silent revolutionaries, enabling movements to organize, disseminate information, and mobilize support on a global scale.

3. Cultural Movements and Identity Politics:

- **Feminist Movements:** The ongoing feminist movements, advocating for gender equality and challenging patriarchal norms, represent silent revolutionaries reshaping political landscapes by influencing policies, discourse, and cultural attitudes.

- **Civil Rights Movements:** Historical civil rights movements, such as the African-American Civil Rights Movement, serve as examples of silent revolutionaries challenging systemic racism and reshaping the political and legal landscape.

4. Environmental Activism and Climate Justice:

- **Global Environmental Movements:** Movements advocating for climate justice and environmental sustainability constitute silent revolutionaries that influence political agendas, policies, and international cooperation.

- **Youth-Led Climate Strikes:** Youth-led climate strikes, epitomized by figures like Greta Thunberg, showcase the power of grassroots movements in compelling political action and shaping the discourse on climate change.

5. Techno-Politics and Cyber Activism:

- **Hacktivism:** Cyber activism, or hacktivism, represents a silent revolutionary force where individuals and groups leverage technology to challenge oppressive regimes, promote transparency, and advocate for human rights.

- **Blockchain and Decentralized Movements:** Technologies like blockchain enable decentralized movements, disrupting traditional power structures and offering new models for governance and political participation.

6. Populism and Anti-Establishment Movements:

- **Rise of Populist Leaders:** Populist movements and leaders, often leveraging economic grievances and nationalist sentiments, act as silent revolutionaries challenging established political norms and reshaping the global political landscape.

- **Anti-Establishment Sentiment:** Movements fueled by anti-establishment sentiment, seen in various regions, reflect a silent revolutionary force challenging political elites and fostering demands for greater accountability.

7. LGBTQ+ Rights Movements:

- **Advocacy for LGBTQ+ Rights:** Silent revolutionaries within LGBTQ+ rights movements have transformed societal attitudes, influenced legal frameworks, and reshaped political landscapes by challenging discriminatory laws and fostering inclusivity.

- **Marriage Equality and Legal Recognition:** Achievements such as marriage equality reflect the impact of silent revolutionaries in reshaping legal frameworks and challenging entrenched social norms.

8. Indigenous Rights Movements:

- **Indigenous Activism:** Movements advocating for indigenous rights, land sovereignty, and cultural preservation serve as silent revolutionaries challenging historical injustices and influencing policies related to indigenous communities.

- **Recognition of Indigenous Knowledge:** Silent revolutionaries within indigenous rights movements contribute to the recognition and integration of indigenous knowledge and perspectives in political decision-making.

9. Economic Movements and Inequality:

- **Occupy Wall Street:** Movements like Occupy Wall Street exemplify silent revolutionaries challenging economic inequalities, corporate power, and advocating for a more equitable distribution of resources.

- **Global Anti-Austerity Protests:** Movements against austerity measures in various countries represent silent revolutionaries demanding economic policies that prioritize social welfare over fiscal consolidation.

10. Anti-Corruption Movements:

- **Transparency and Accountability:** Silent revolutionaries within anti-corruption movements seek to establish transparency and accountability in governance, influencing political structures and fostering a culture of integrity.

- **Role of Whistleblowers:** Whistleblowers, acting as silent revolutionaries, play a crucial role in exposing corruption and triggering political reforms by bringing hidden information to light.

11. Post-Colonial Movements and National Identity:

- **Movements for Independence:** Post-colonial movements that led to the decolonization of nations represent silent revolutionaries reshaping political landscapes by redefining national identities and challenging imperialistic structures.

- **Cultural Renaissance:** Movements fostering cultural renaissance post-colonization serve as silent revolutionaries in reclaiming indigenous identities and shaping inclusive national narratives.

12. Human Rights Advocacy:

- **International Human Rights Movements:** Silent revolutionaries within human rights movements influence global political norms, challenging authoritarian regimes, advocating for justice, and shaping international policies.

- **Role of NGOs and Advocacy Groups:** Non-governmental organizations (NGOs) and advocacy groups act as silent revolutionaries, providing a platform for grassroots movements and influencing political agendas.

13. Urbanization and the Politics of Cities:

- **Urban Movements:** As the world becomes more urbanized, silent revolutionaries in urban movements influence local and national politics, advocating for sustainable development, social justice, and community empowerment.

- **City Diplomacy:** Cities increasingly engage in diplomacy, forming networks and alliances that influence global politics, showcasing the evolving role of urban centers as silent revolutionaries in the political landscape.

14. Public Health Advocacy and Global Crises:

- **Pandemic Response Movements:** Movements advocating for global health, exemplified during the COVID-19 pandemic, serve as silent revolutionaries shaping political responses, public health policies, and international cooperation.

- **Access to Medicines Campaigns:** Advocacy for affordable and accessible medicines reflects silent revolutionaries challenging pharmaceutical policies and influencing political decisions related to public health.

15. Education and Knowledge Movements:

- **Open Access and Education for All:** Movements advocating for open access to information, affordable education, and knowledge-sharing represent silent revolutionaries fostering informed citizenry and influencing policies related to education.

- **Online Learning and Digital Literacy:** The digital transformation in education serves as a silent revolutionary force, reshaping learning paradigms and influencing the politics of knowledge dissemination.

16. Futurism and Political Imagination:

- **Futurist Movements:** Movements envisioning alternative political futures, influenced by technological advancements and changing societal values, act as silent revolutionaries challenging established norms and shaping political discourse.

- **Speculative Fiction and Political Ideas:** Works of speculative fiction contribute to the political imagination, influencing how societies envision and articulate their political aspirations, serving as silent revolutionaries in shaping future possibilities.

17. Diaspora Movements and Transnational Advocacy:

- **Diaspora Activism:** Movements led by diaspora communities serve as silent revolutionaries by engaging in transnational advocacy, influencing policies in their countries of origin, and contributing to global conversations.

- **Digital Diaspora Activism:** The digital connectivity of diaspora communities facilitates transnational activism, allowing individuals to mobilize and advocate for political causes across borders.

18. Challenges Faced by Silent Revolutionaries:

- **Repression and Backlash:** Silent revolutionaries often face repression, censorship, and backlash from entrenched political interests, requiring resilience and strategic adaptation to navigate hostile environments.

- **Fragmentation and Co-Optation:** Internal divisions and co-optation by political actors pose challenges to the effectiveness of silent revolutionaries, requiring movements to address internal dynamics and maintain their original objectives.

19. The Future of Silent Revolutionaries:

- **Hybrid Activism:** The future of silent revolutionaries may witness hybrid forms of activism, blending online and offline strategies to navigate evolving political landscapes.

- **Intersectionality and Collaborative Movements:**

Movements that embrace intersectionality and collaboration across diverse social issues are likely to shape the future of silent revolutionaries, fostering solidarity and collective impact.

Conclusion: The influence of silent revolutionaries in shaping political landscapes is profound and enduring. Whether driven by technological advancements, cultural shifts, or grassroots activism, these movements challenge established norms, redefine political narratives, and contribute to the ongoing evolution of global governance. Understanding the dynamics of silent revolutionaries is essential for policymakers, scholars, and citizens alike, as it offers insights into the undercurrents that shape the political trajectories of societies across the world. As silent revolutionaries continue to emerge, adapt, and transform, their impact on the political landscape will be a defining force in the unfolding narrative of human societies and their quest for justice, equality, and progressive change.

CHAPTER 40: RESILIENCE IN SILENCE: NAVIGATING THE UNPREDICTABLE IN GEOPOLITICS

In the intricate dance of global affairs, the concept of "Resilience in Silence" emerges as a nuanced approach to navigating the unpredictable currents of geopolitics. This entails the ability of nations, leaders, and diplomatic entities to adapt, endure, and strategize effectively in the face of unforeseen challenges without necessarily broadcasting their every move. This comprehensive exploration delves into historical contexts, contemporary examples, and the underlying principles that define resilience in silence, unraveling the complexities of maneuvering through the unpredictable terrain of geopolitics.

1. Historical Foundations of Resilience in Silence:

- **Diplomacy in Ancient Civilizations:** Historical civilizations, such as ancient China and Rome, employed silent diplomacy and strategic ambiguity to navigate alliances, rivalries, and power dynamics.

- **Quiet Alliances in World Wars:** During the World Wars, silent alliances and covert operations showcased the importance of resilience in silence as nations sought to outmaneuver adversaries without revealing their full strategies.

2. The Art of Strategic Ambiguity:

- **Cold War Diplomacy:** The Cold War era exemplified the art of strategic ambiguity, with nations like the United States and the Soviet Union employing a balance of silence and signaling to prevent miscalculations.

- **Ambiguous Nuclear Posture:** Nuclear-armed nations maintain deliberate ambiguity about their nuclear postures, utilizing silence as a tool to deter potential adversaries.

3. Crisis Management and Silent Resilience:

- **Cuban Missile Crisis:** The Cuban Missile Crisis serves as a historical case where silent resilience played a pivotal role, as leaders navigated a delicate situation without escalating it into a full-blown conflict.

- **Diplomatic Backchannels:** Silent crisis management often involves diplomatic backchannels, allowing nations to communicate discreetly during tense moments to avoid public escalation.

4. Economic Resilience in Silence:

- **Currency Wars:** Nations engage in silent economic strategies, such as currency interventions, without overtly declaring their intentions to maintain economic resilience.

- **Trade Negotiations Behind Closed Doors:** Silent negotiations in trade agreements and economic partnerships demonstrate how nations protect their economic interests without exposing vulnerabilities.

5. Intelligence and Covert Operations:

- **Espionage during the Cold War:** The Cold War saw extensive silent operations by intelligence agencies, highlighting the role of covert actions in gathering information and influencing geopolitical outcomes.

- **Cyber Espionage:** In the digital age, cyber espionage has become a silent tool for nations to gather intelligence, disrupt adversaries, and maintain a covert advantage.

6. Silent Resilience in Proxy Conflicts:

- **Proxy Wars during the Cold War:** Superpowers engaged in proxy conflicts, employing silent resilience by supporting allies without direct involvement to avoid open confrontation.

- **Contemporary Proxy Conflicts:** Current examples, like conflicts in the Middle East, showcase silent resilience in navigating complex geopolitical landscapes through support for proxy actors.

7. Multilateral Diplomacy and Silent Collaboration:

- **UN Security Council Diplomacy:** Silent collaboration within the United Nations Security Council involves negotiations, compromises, and strategic positioning by member states to achieve geopolitical objectives.

- **Informal Alliances:** Nations often form informal alliances without public declarations, relying on silent collaboration to advance shared interests in multilateral forums.

8. Climate Diplomacy and Silent Agreements:

- **Paris Agreement Negotiations:** Climate diplomacy involves silent resilience, with nations negotiating behind closed doors to reach agreements on emissions reductions, adaptation strategies, and climate finance.

- **Covert Environmental Security Measures:** Nations may implement covert measures to address environmental security threats without overtly revealing their strategies.

9. Silent Responses to Hybrid Threats:

- **Hybrid Warfare Tactics:** Nations facing hybrid threats, including cyber-attacks, disinformation campaigns, and unconventional tactics, respond with silent resilience by adapting strategies without necessarily publicizing their countermeasures.

- **Grey Zone Conflicts:** Silent resilience is crucial in navigating grey zone conflicts, where activities fall between traditional war and peace, requiring adaptive and nuanced responses.

10. Leadership and Crisis Communication:

- **Leadership Resilience:** Leaders exhibit resilience in silence by carefully managing crisis communication, balancing transparency with the need to withhold sensitive information during emergencies.

- **Strategic Silence:** Choosing when to remain silent is a strategic leadership decision, as leaders navigate crises and unforeseen challenges while projecting stability and control.

11. Cultural and Soft Power Resilience:

- **Cultural Diplomacy:** Nations utilize cultural exchanges and soft power initiatives as silent tools to enhance their global influence without resorting to overt displays of strength.

- **Public Diplomacy:** Silent resilience extends to public diplomacy, where nations shape narratives, perceptions, and reputations through strategic communication without engaging in direct confrontation.

12. Global Health Crisis Management:

- **Pandemic Responses:** Silent resilience is evident in global responses to health crises, with nations coordinating behind the scenes to manage pandemics, share resources, and mitigate the impact without causing panic.

- **Vaccine Diplomacy:** Nations engage in silent vaccine diplomacy, strategically distributing vaccines to enhance their geopolitical influence and strengthen international partnerships.

13. Adaptability in Geoeconomics:

- **Changing Economic Alliances:** Nations display resilience in silence by adapting economic strategies, forming and dissolving alliances based on shifting geopolitical dynamics, and safeguarding economic interests without overt declarations.

- **Silent Trade Wars:** Geoeconomic resilience involves nations engaging in silent trade wars, implementing tariffs, and maneuvering within international economic systems without overtly signaling their intentions.

14. Silent Resilience in the Cyber Domain:

- **Cybersecurity Strategies:** Silent resilience in cyberspace involves nations developing robust cybersecurity strategies, adapting to evolving threats, and countering cyber-attacks without necessarily publicizing their defensive capabilities.

- **Strategic Silence in Cyber Conflicts:** Nations may strategically remain silent about their involvement in cyber conflicts to maintain ambiguity and avoid escalation.

15. Global Governance and Silent Influence:

- **UN Security Council Dynamics:** Silent influence within the UN Security Council involves nations leveraging their positions, forming alliances, and utilizing strategic silence to shape resolutions and decisions.

- **Quiet Diplomacy in International Organizations:** Nations exercise silent resilience in international organizations by influencing policies and decisions through quiet diplomacy, strategic alliances, and discreet negotiations.

16. The Role of Think Tanks and Non-State Actors:

- **Think Tank Influence:** Think tanks and non-state actors contribute to silent resilience by shaping policy debates, conducting research, and influencing political agendas behind the scenes.

- **NGOs and Grassroots Movements:** Non-governmental

organizations and grassroots movements act as silent resilience agents, advocating for change, influencing public opinion, and pressuring governments without overt displays of power.

17. Challenges to Silent Resilience:

- **Information Warfare:** The era of information warfare poses challenges to silent resilience, as disinformation, propaganda, and manipulation threaten the ability of nations to navigate geopolitical challenges discreetly.

- **Transparency and Accountability:** Balancing the need for strategic silence with transparency and accountability poses a challenge, as overly secretive actions can lead to distrust and geopolitical tensions.

18. Ethical Considerations in Silent Resilience:

- **Human Rights Concerns:** The ethical dimensions of silent resilience come to the forefront in situations involving human rights abuses, as nations grapple with balancing strategic imperatives with moral responsibilities.

- **Environmental and Social Impact:** Silent strategies in geopolitical maneuvers must consider the potential environmental and social impacts, requiring a delicate balance between national interests and global well-being.

19. Future Trajectories of Silent Resilience:

- **Technological Advances:** The future of silent resilience will be shaped by technological advances, including artificial intelligence, quantum computing, and advanced surveillance capabilities, influencing how nations navigate geopolitical challenges.

- **Global Governance Reforms:** The evolution of global governance structures and reforms will impact how nations exercise silent resilience in international relations, emphasizing the need for adaptability and collaboration.

Conclusion: "Resilience in Silence" stands as a dynamic and adaptive approach to navigating the unpredictable currents of geopolitics. Whether in crisis management, economic strategies, or global governance, the ability to exhibit silent resilience is a hallmark of strategic acumen. As the world continues to face unprecedented challenges, understanding and mastering the art of resilience in silence will be essential for nations, leaders, and diplomatic entities seeking to safeguard their interests, mitigate risks, and thrive in an ever-evolving geopolitical landscape.

EPILOGUE

As we conclude our exploration into the clandestine world of silent diplomacy, we find ourselves at the crossroads of understanding and intrigue. The journey through these pages has been a revelation, unraveling the hidden forces that silently shape the world's geopolitical landscape. From the covert alliances of ancient civilizations to the cybernetic frontiers of the modern era, the tapestry of silent diplomacy has been laid bare.

In reflecting upon the chapters that have unfolded, we recognize the enduring nature of silent forces throughout history. The echoes of past conflicts, the legacy of diplomatic strategies employed in the shadows, and the persistent impact of historical events collectively weave the intricate fabric of global dynamics. The chessboard of geopolitics, marked by unspoken agreements, covert alliances, and strategic silences, emerges as a stage where nations dance to the subtle rhythm of power and influence.

As we consider the challenges faced by silent diplomacy, from the ethical considerations surrounding covert operations to the ever-present specter of information warfare, the complexities of navigating the unseen become even more apparent. The delicate balance between strategic silence and transparency, the resilience required to weather unexpected crises, and the adaptability demanded in a rapidly evolving world underscore the artistry of silent diplomacy.

This exploration has also shed light on the diverse actors

shaping global affairs. From intelligence agencies and non-state actors to international organizations and individuals influencing policy, the ensemble of players on the geopolitical stage is vast and dynamic. Each contributes to the symphony of silent diplomacy, where every gesture, every decision, resonates in the corridors of power.

As we gaze toward the future, we recognize the evolving nature of silent diplomacy in the face of technological advancements, shifting power dynamics, and the emergence of new global challenges. The geopolitical landscape is in constant flux, demanding a nimble and strategic approach from those who seek to navigate its intricacies. The silent revolutionaries, movements shaping political landscapes, and the resilient forces at play in geopolitics all point to a world where adaptability and foresight are paramount.

In concluding this journey, we invite readers to reflect on the lessons learned within these pages. The understanding that diplomatic interactions extend far beyond the public eye, the recognition that the echoes of history persist in shaping contemporary affairs, and the awareness of the hidden influencers on the global stage—all contribute to a more nuanced comprehension of the world's geopolitical complexities.

"Silent Diplomacy: Hidden Forces Shaping the World" is not merely a book; it is an invitation to become astute observers of the silent dance that shapes our world. It is a call to recognize the forces at play beneath the surface, a reminder that the silent handshake echoes louder than the spoken word, and an opportunity to comprehend the complex symphony of global affairs.

As we part ways with this exploration, let us carry with us the knowledge that the unseen horizons of silent diplomacy continue to unfold. The journey does not end here but extends into the uncharted territories of future geopolitics, where the silent forces we have unraveled will continue to shape the destiny of nations and define the course of history.

May this book serve as a guide for those seeking to navigate the unseen currents, a source of inspiration for the silent architects crafting the geopolitical landscape, and a testament to the enduring influence of silent diplomacy in an ever-changing world. The journey into the unseen has just begun, and the horizons ahead are rich with the promise of discovery, adaptation, and understanding.

The End.